Rax Me That Buik

HIGHLIGHTS FROM THE COLLECTIONS OF THE NATIONAL LIBRARY OF SCOTLAND

IAIN GORDON BROWN

SCALA

To my curatorial colleagues
in the National Library of Scotland,
past and present, living and dead,
in gratitude for
friendship, inspiration and scholarship,
1977-2010

ABOVE: Dominie Sampson in a state of ecstasy in the
library at Woodbourne. Frontispiece illustration by
C.R. Leslie to the first volume of Scott's *Guy Mannering*
in the 'Magnum' edition of the Waverley Novels, 1829

Contents

Introduction

THE TITLE OF THIS ANTHOLOGY of highlights from the National Library of Scotland's collections needs some explanation. The motto 'Rax Me That Buik' was granted with its coat of arms (Fig. 1) in 1953 to the Scottish Central Library for Students. This was subsumed into the National Library of Scotland in 1974 as a Lending Services division. The old SCL building in Edinburgh's Lawnmarket, part of the historic Royal Mile leading to the Castle, now serves as the administrative headquarters of the National Library and the motto is carved over the door. It is

Fig. 1

derived from a remark made in the General Assembly of the Church of Scotland in 1796 by a minister wanting a Bible to which to refer. In Scots, *rax* means 'reach', or 'hand' me, and the motto may be read as a generalised request for 'buiks' (Scots for books) of all ages and kinds as containers of information, and indeed for access to recorded knowledge as a whole. It is the National Library's business to provide such information, based upon the historical record of Scotland and the Scottish people – in its reading-rooms, by answering enquiries of all sorts, by means of exhibitions and through public programmes, in publications, and (increasingly) over networks and through digital resources – to the people of Scotland and, beyond, to all interested throughout the world. Our 'public' is all those who need to consult, directly or remotely, the accumulated collections of 330 years which document the life and learning of Scotland in all its aspects.

This book presents a selection of the 'Scottish' collections of the Library, defined in the broadest sense. Even within these parameters, we can barely begin to appreciate the astonishing riches of such extensive and diverse holdings, and inevitably this volume contains only a tiny sampling. But the selection has been very carefully considered and structured, and is presented in sectional

Fig. 2

themes which reflect not just aspects of Scottish life and thought, but also areas in which the Library's collections are strongly focused and our holdings world-class. The book, moreover, represents a single curator's personal selection; the themes offer but one of many possible interpretations of the collections.

The National Library, incomparably the largest and finest library in Scotland, works on two distinct levels. It holds the Scottish national collection of printed books and periodicals on all topics, constituting the principal research resource, for example, of works on Spanish literature or Italian art, Egyptology or Islamic studies. And it is also the Scottish nation's 'memory' of its own achievements in every field, through all time, both at home and abroad, and in every corner of the world.

The focus of this book, however, is on 'highlights' rather than 'treasures': fascinating, intriguing and historically significant printed books, manuscripts, maps, music and ephemera. Some of these may be surprising in a national collection, or may not be well known or immediately identifiable as overtly or essentially 'Scottish', whereas many of the Library's absolute 'treasures' are widely known. For the purposes of this volume, it is perhaps of greater importance and interest that we have the Minto Papers, which shed so much light on two significant periods of Indian imperial administration a century apart, or that we continue to acquire the letters and papers of Sir Walter Scott or the Victorian painter David Roberts, having begun to collect in those two areas in 1850 and 1935 respectively.

The National Library was established only in 1925, by the transfer to the state of all the non-legal collections of the historic Advocates' Library, in what was arguably the greatest act of munificence in library history. From modest beginnings in 1680, as the

Fig. 3

Fig. 4

private property of the Faculty of Advocates (the Scottish Bar), that library had grown to be a national institution in all but name. Almost from the outset, it was seen as more than a working legal library; advocates were the most learned men of the nation, and the library reflected their interests in history, antiquities, heraldry and genealogy (Fig.2). Its founder, Sir George Mackenzie of Rosehaugh, called it grandiloquently, in his 1689 Latin inaugural oration, 'this Parnassus and bosom of the muses'. It was widely regarded as the *de facto* 'national library' of Scotland, and its collections, and the men who, in various capacities, looked after them, were of international renown: these included Thomas Ruddiman, David Hume, Adam Ferguson, James Boswell and Walter Scott, who described the Library in 1824 as 'more than princely'.

Over the course of its independent existence the Advocates' Library had acquired great treasures, such as the Pont, Gordon and Adair maps, accessioned before 1742; the Chepman and Myllar prints (the first specimens of Scottish printing, Fig. 3) in 1788; and the superb illuminated manuscript copy of Justinian's 'Institutes' (Fig. 4) in 1831. Manuscripts, indeed, had been acquired as a matter of deliberate policy almost from the start, with the first major purchase being made in 1698. The Copyright Act of 1710, which was applied to the library, led to a substantial and enduring stream of new British publications free of charge. The comparatively meagre funds available could therefore be spent on more exotic items, such as the foreign *belles lettres* proposed by David Hume, who established a fine tradition of such acquisition which is still

maintained, or the older 'antiquarian' and scholarly material in all fields (scientific as well as humane) which characterised the Library's accession policy from the start. The tradition of collecting the papers of individual Scots, now such a distinctive feature and glory of the National Library, has its origins as long ago as 1706.

The history of the Advocates' Library between the early eighteenth century and the mid-nineteenth was bedevilled by a series of false hopes for a suitable building to house a collection of increasing size and importance. A splendid library palace designed by Robert Adam in 1791 remained unbuilt; the glorious Upper Signet Library, perhaps the most elegant public space in Edinburgh, was disposed of in 1826 as inadequate for the expanding needs of the collection; and of the vast new library designed by William Henry Playfair, only a very small part was actually built in 1830, and even this remained incomplete for many years. Further expansion proved impossible and this, together with the ever-increasing burden on a private body of maintaining a *de facto* national institution without public aid, hastened the inevitable transfer to the state. In the 1870s Thomas Carlyle testified not only to the Library's exceptional quality but to its 'national' status as a vital resource for scholarship in Scotland, suggesting that its anomalous position should be rectified by 'whatever calls itself a Government in that country'.

The transitional period between 'private' and fully-public institution was marked by a series of highly significant donations: for example, the purchase in 1913 by an American

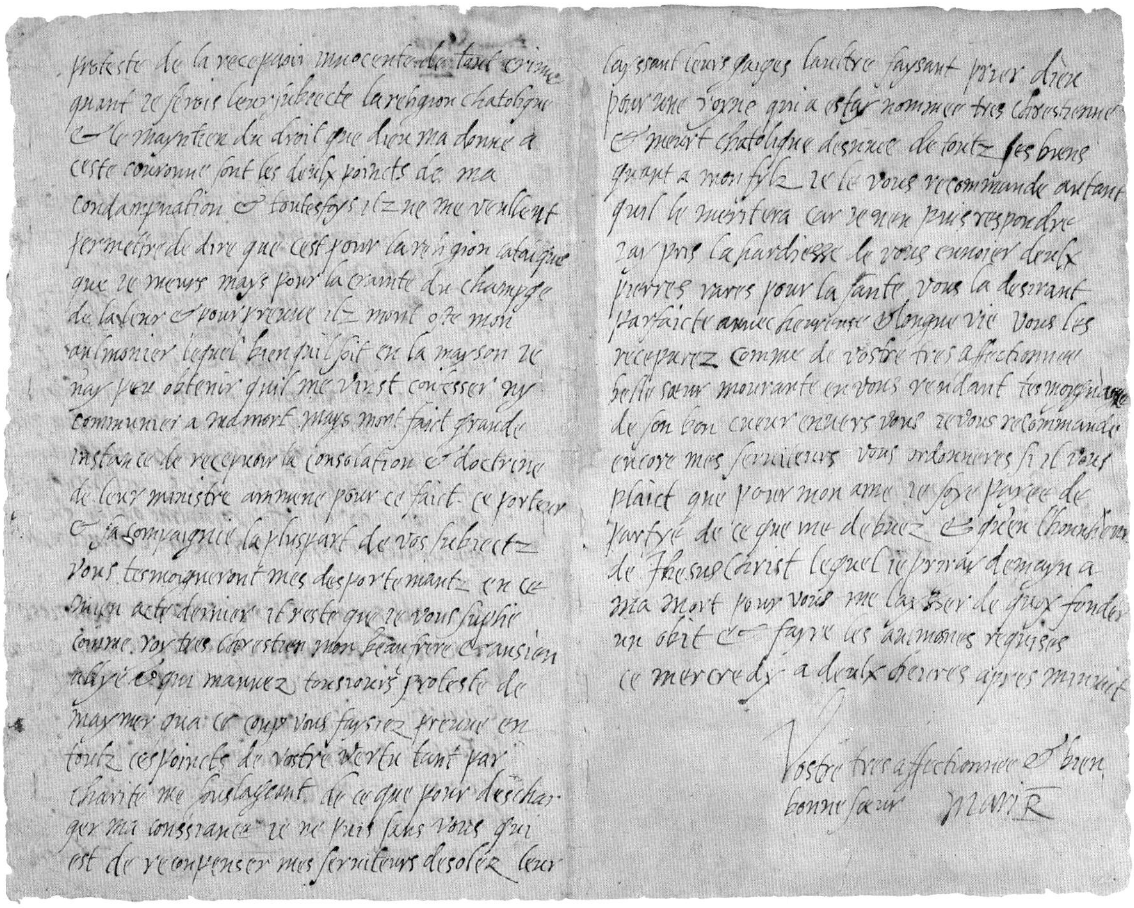

Fig. 5

Fig. 6

benefactor of the Glenriddell Burns Manuscripts, and their donation to a trust 'for the Scottish people, for ever', established until a national library for Scotland should be founded. The manuscripts came to the new institution in 1926. The last letter of Mary, Queen of Scots (Fig. 5), was similarly saved by a group of subscribers in 1918 and was given to the Advocates' Library in 1923, when a national future was assured.

The new national institution needed to be adequately accommodated. The generosity of Sir Alexander Grant, a rich biscuit manufacturer, made possible not only the transfer of collections from the private to the public realm, but also the construction of a new building, with matching government funding. But there followed a long and vigorous debate about suitable site and style, neither of which were well chosen. The Library's main building on George IV Bridge was described by its own architect as exuding 'an air of frigid serenity'. Begun in 1937, but with work suspended for the duration of the war and for some time afterwards, the building was opened only in 1956 (Fig.6). By the 1970s a major additional site was already being planned, a mile to the south in Newington. Here in 1989 (with a second phase in 1995), a large, new, high-tech building was opened to house an expanded Map Library, the then Scottish Science Library, staff accommodation and very extensive stackage, much of it subterranean. Although the original main

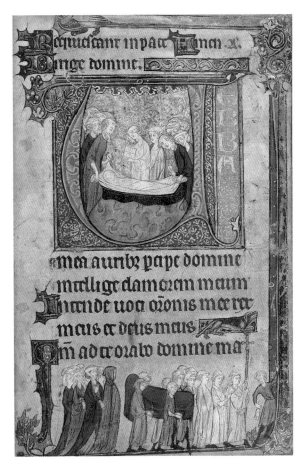

Fig. 7

Fig. 8

building still contains millions of general collection books in the humanities, on its seven stack-floors below the level of George IV Bridge, it is increasingly regarded as a 'heritage' building. It holds the manuscript and older book collections and provides the location for exhibitions and the majority of public functions, with new visitor facilities opened in 2009.

Since 1925, innumerable benefactions and donations have been made to the National Library, some of exceptional value and significance and all enhancing beyond measure the international prestige and scholarly standing of the institution. A vigorous purchasing policy has also been pursued. Every year has brought new treasures. The Bute Collection of English Plays, for example, was bought in 1956. The Newhailes Library and papers were allocated to the Library by the Treasury in 1978. The year 1986 stands out as especially remarkable, with the acquisition of the late thirteenth-century Murthly Book of Hours (Fig.7); the Pforzheimer Scott Manuscripts, repatriated from New York; and the Interleaved Set of the Waverley Novels, used by Walter Scott (Fig.8) in the preparation of his final edition, also brought home after exile in the US. That year, too, the Norris of Speke Collection, otherwise known through their Scottish provenance as the Cambuskenneth Books, looted from Edinburgh as war booty by an English knight at the sack of the city in

1544, were 'repatriated' from Liverpool on a temporary basis. This collection of sixteenth-century law books was later bought by the Library. And in 2006, the John Murray Archive crowned the better part of a century's worth of acquisitions in the field of publishing history as the single most important such literary archive in existence, and by far the Library's most expensive acquisition in its long history.

The National Library of Scotland has developed into one of the great libraries of Europe, combining distinguished holdings on every conceivable topic with general collections accumulated as a result of the legal deposit privilege granted in 1710. Elements of its huge stock, however – notably its vast and diverse manuscript and map collections, and its rich holdings of older books and special printed collections acquired by purchase, gift and deposit – place the institution in a different league, as one of the great research libraries of the world. The Library is a treasure-house of material written or printed in Scotland, by and about Scotland and the Scots, and relating to Scottish enterprise in every field, throughout the world and over the centuries. It constitutes the primary research resource for the study of Scottish history, literature, arts, sciences, intellectual and social life, popular culture, exploration, imperial administration, the Scottish diaspora and the world-wide activities of Scots.

Land, Landscape and Topographical Record

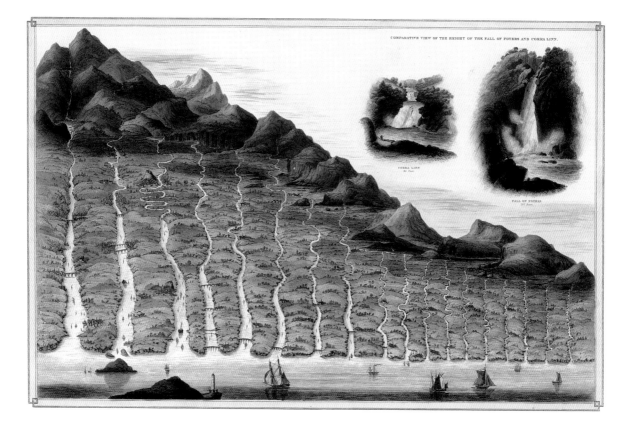

1.1 Land of the mountain and the flood

SIR WALTER SCOTT, to paraphrase the clerihew, invented a lot. In the first of his series of narrative poems, *The Lay of the Last Minstrel* (1805), he coined a description of Scotland that has held fast in the imagination of succeeding generations. Canto VI contains the famous lines:

> O Caledonia! stern and wild,
> Meet nurse for a poetic child!
> Land of brown heath and shaggy wood
> Land of the mountain and the flood...

The composer Hamish MacCunn adopted the last phrase as title for his celebrated overture of 1887. The year of Scott's death, 1832, saw the publication by John Thomson of the most ambitious of the several atlases he brought out. Though its production ruined him financially, Thomson's *Atlas of Scotland* was a milestone in the long and distinguished history of Scottish cartography. The fine maps were accompanied by a 'Memoir of the Geography of Scotland', vividly illustrated with two dramatic plates demonstrating the comparative heights of the mountains and the lengths of the rivers. That of the rivers (drawn and engraved by William Home Lizars) is shown here, their courses snaking inland as if all run to the same sea-board. Edinburgh and Stirling castles are distinct landmarks on the un-bridged Forth between the Bass Rock and the foothills of the Highland mountains.

JOHN THOMSON, *The Atlas of Scotland, Containing Maps of Each County* (Edinburgh, 1832) EMS.s.712

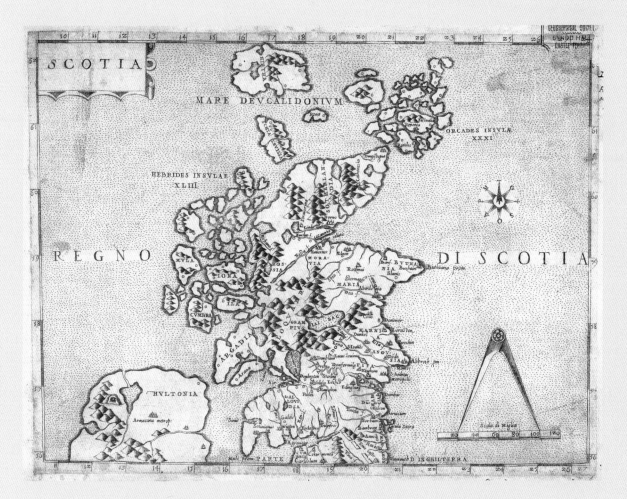

1.2 **A Venetian view of Scotia**

THIS FIRST SURVIVING printed map of Scotland shows it as a political and geographical realm 'entire of itself' and isolated from its southern neighbour – though not entirely from Ireland – and from the continent of Europe. It is attributed to the Venetian engraver Paolo Forlani, who was active between 1558 and 1571. Venetian sailors, navigators and map-makers, some of the ablest in the world, clearly knew little of the genuine outline of the rugged Scottish coast and the myriad islands of the north and west. The map is derived from an earlier sixteenth-century prototype which shows Scotland as part of the British Isles. The choice of place-names is drawn from those in Hector Boece's Latin history of Scotland, published in Paris in 1527 and translated into

Scots by John Bellenden about 1536. Dependence on literary sources is reflected in the prominence given to (and therefore magnification of) localities mentioned in contemporary written accounts. There are striking distortions of scale: the vast Loch Tay ('Tai Lac'), and an astonishingly huge 'Hirta' or St Kilda at the top, shifted to the north from the far west. Loch Lomond's islands make it resemble some sort of fruit loaf. Kintyre and especially Iona are enormously inflated. The distinctive shape of Skye is lost among a cluster of isles posing as the Hebrides. The capital city has the spelling, 'Edingburg', which still bedevils correspondence from foreigners, and even English people who should know better.

Scotia. Regno di Scotia (?Venice, c.1570) EMS.s.6A

1.3 Scotland as caricature

THE DISTINCTIVE OUTLINE of Scotland has lent itself, especially in the Victorian period, to several amusing depictions of the land, with its jagged coastline and interestingly shaped islands, as a caricature or as combinations of characters. A number of such representations are in the Library's collections, embodying what were regarded as traditional Scottish 'types'. The piper's wind-blown kilt and plaid, and his drones with their ribbons, might usefully form parts of an indented coast. The fishwife with her creel or basket (so memorably photographed by D.O. Hill and Robert Adamson at Newhaven in the dawn of the age of photography) might similarly do duty as an adaptable element of landscape. This appealing example, by the great Edinburgh cartographic firm of John Bartholomew & Son, is particularly effective because more restrained and subtle than some. It was produced as an advertisement for a hotel company, the Edinburgh and Glasgow premises of which appear in three corners. One of the woman's creel-load of fishes appears to have escaped, and to have been press-ganged into service to form the Outer Hebrides.

Philip's Comic Map of Scotland (Edinburgh, 1882)
Bartholomew Archive, Acc. 10222/PR/5.f.33

1.4 Geology and scenery

John Clerk of Eldin was one of the great men of the Scottish Enlightenment. He came of a distinguished Midlothian family prominent in the arts and sciences, and was himself a successful coal-owner. His major achievements were as an amateur in the diverse fields of etching, geology and naval tactics (cf. 4.11). This is one of his finest plates. Dating from 1774, it represents Arthur's Seat and the prospect of Edinburgh looking south from Lochend. Technically it is quite advanced, with an attempt made to render reflections in the water. Wild-fowlers add life and drama in the foreground. More than a purely topographical record, the plate shows Clerk's interest in, and understanding of, the geological structure of the city. Clerk was a close friend of James Hutton, and worked with him on the illustration of Hutton's seminal *Theory of the Earth*. The extinct volcano of Arthur's Seat and the Salisbury Crags were to become classic geological localities where Hutton's revolutionary theories were worked out and illustrated. Professor John Playfair praised Clerk's zeal in 'studying the surface no less than the interior of the earth; his extensive information in most branches of natural history…' In this remarkable view, science and art are united. Clerk's friend Paul Sandby showed such picturesque images as this to fellow English artists, and reported that they were 'wonderfully struck… they conceive [Edinburgh] to be one of the most Romantic cities in the world'.

Etchings, Chiefly of Views in Scotland. By John Clerk, Esq., of Eldin. MDCCLXXIII-MDCCLXXIX (Edinburgh, 1825)
ABS.10.92.4

1.5 And did those feet…

Sir William Jardine of Applegirth, a Dumfriesshire baronet, was a distinguished naturalist who is best remembered as the editor of the Naturalist's Library, a series of popular books to which he himself contributed many volumes. His own scientific interests ranged over geology, botany, anatomy, ornithology and ichthyology. Confusingly, in view of this last (which is, of course, the study of fish) he was also concerned with the study of fossil footprints, or ichnology. On this somewhat recherché topic he published an enormous three-part folio based on his observations at the Corncockle quarry, Lochmaben, where a remarkable series of reptilian labyrinthodont footprints was discovered. These prehistoric animals had left impressions on wet ground which had been covered by windblown sand and preserved in the rock which then formed. Jardine enlisted the services of his brother-in-law, the distinguished engraver William Home Lizars, both to lithograph the illustrations for his book and to publish what must have been a commercially risky work. Huge bistre plates reproduce at life size both the footprints, and apparently transient features such as raindrops, which Jardine showed could also be 'fossilised' – surely the first record of such a characteristic manifestation of the Scottish climate. The Library's copy was given by Jardine to his second wife Hyacinthe Symonds in 1872, shortly after their marriage – one of the more unusual and eccentric matrimonial gifts that a curator is likely to come across.

Sir William Jardine, *The Ichnology of Annandale or Illustrations of Footprints Impressed on the New Red Sandstone of Corncockle Muir* (Edinburgh, 1851-53)
EL.4.88.27

1.6 'A chield's among you, taking notes...'

THIS CHARMING WATERCOLOUR by C.J. Harford illustrates an important antiquarian alliance. The figure with the parasol is Adam Mansfeldt de Cardonnel (later Cardonnel-Lawson), the other Francis Grose, sketchbook in hand. A servant brings an artefact for their attention. The scene is the mighty ruin of Tantallon Castle, East Lothian, with its distinctive curtain wall across a headland. Grose, an English captain of militia and devotee of medieval architecture, is celebrated for his *Antiquities of England and Wales* and equally for the *Antiquities of Scotland*, which was the result of his three antiquarian tours of the country in 1788, 1789 and 1790. On the second of these he met Robert Burns, and extracted from him verses designed to accompany a plate of Alloway Kirk: thus did 'Tam o'Shanter' come

to be written. Burns's verses to Grose himself are celebrated; and Burns also said that he had 'never seen a man of more original observation, anecdote and remark'. Cardonnel accompanied Grose on his Scottish archaeological expeditions. As this drawing shows, Grose was short and stocky and Cardonnel tall and spare: they might almost be the eponymous 'fat and the lean Antiquarians' of Grose's own caricature drawing published in his *Antiquarian Repertory*. Cardonnel published antiquarian and numismatic works including *Picturesque Antiquities of Scotland* (1788-93). The Library holds what appears to be Cardonnel's only surviving antiquarian album of prints and drawings. It was evidently one of a series, previously unknown to scholarship. This watercolour comes from it.
Acc. 12139

1.7 Recording the heritage

AT FIRST GLANCE this watercolour by James Drummond, done in 1848, might be taken to represent restorers at work, or architectural historians surveying in Trinity College Kirk, Edinburgh. The men are in fact recording and numbering mouldings, prior to the demolition that year of the finest collegiate church of late medieval Scotland. The land had been bought by the North British Railway Company. The stones were laid aside, but were pilfered for building materials and garden ornaments. Lord Cockburn condemned 'an outrage by sordid traders virtually consented to by a tasteless city and sanctioned by an insensible Parliament…These people would remove Pompeii for a railway and tell us they had applied it to better purpose in Dundee'. The rump of the church was subsequently re-erected on a neighbouring site. The Library's collections of topographical drawings and of material relating to the antiquarian

record of Scotland are large, varied and distinguished. The fundamental assemblage of papers of Sir Robert Sibbald was bought by the Faculty of Advocates in 1723. George Paton's extensive papers, including correspondence with Thomas Pennant and Richard Gough, entered the collections in 1816. The drawings of Lieutenant-General George Henry Hutton were acquired in 1851, Hutton's antiquarian correspondence having been purchased in 1829. Many other antiquarian collections have been added since. The Ross Drawings, from which this watercolour comes, is by far the largest: an assemblage of more than 7000 drawings, prints and notes by (or collected by) the historians of Scottish baronial, castellated and ecclesiastical architecture, David MacGibbon and Thomas Ross, presented in 1931.
MS. 689, no. 24

State and Law 2

2.1 'The meteor flag of England' – and of Scotland too

THE NATIONAL FLAG of Scotland is the saltire cross of St Andrew, white or silver (argent) on a blue (azure) field. As a result of the Union of the Crowns in 1603 it became necessary to design a new flag (initially for naval use) that would express the concept of a united kingdom. A commission was established under Charles, first Earl of Nottingham (formerly Lord Howard of Effingham, Lord High Admiral, and hero of the defeat of the Spanish Armada). The designs shown here are for various schemes by which the ensigns of the two countries of England and Scotland might be combined. None is entirely satisfactory. One may believe that the Union Flag or 'Union Jack' which did in the end come into being

(itself to be modified again nearly two centuries later on the union with Ireland) was a happier solution to a pretty intractable problem, involving a delicate compromise of national pride and prominence, as well as aesthetics. In the seventeenth century, a version of the Union Flag showing the saltire overlying the red St George's cross may have been used semi-officially in Scotland. Lord Nottingham has annotated the middle design of the lower register, which shows the two flags impaling each other, with a succinct comment of approval: 'In my poure opinion this wyll be the most fetest, for this is like man and wife wtout blemesh on to other.'

MS. 2517, f. 67

2.2 'The ruddy lion ramping in his field of tressured gold'

THE ROYAL ARMS or 'Ensigns of Dominion and Sovereignty' of the king of Scots indicated official power and symbolised government authority. Today the arms, quartered with those of England and Ireland, form the familiar royal arms we see on everyday objects such as our passports. A special quartered version, giving added prominence to the Scottish element, is used officially by government in Scotland. But the old royal banner and arms continue to be sanctioned for use by certain officers of state; these arms appear at the opening of John Bellenden's translation of Hector Boece's history of Scotland, printed in Edinburgh, by Thomas Davidson, 'prenter to the kyngis nobyll grace', about 1540. The original Latin work had been published in Paris in 1527: both are fine examples of early printing. Bellenden's translation has the further distinction of being the earliest example of Scottish printed prose. The arms shown are those of James V. The achievement incorporates all significant elements of Scottish national symbolism: lions (on shield and as crest); unicorns bearing national flags; thistles (in the collar encircling the shield, and strewn about); the suspended St Andrew jewel; the '*In Defens*' motto. All that is lacking is the motto (later usually found on the compartment upon which the supporters stand) *Nemo Me Impune Lacessit* ('no one assails me with impunity'), the proud and ancient boast of Scotland, her state institutions, her regiments and (more usually in the dialect form of 'Wha daur meddle wi' me') her sometimes prickly citizenry.

HECTOR BOECE, translated by Johne Bellenden, *Heir Beginnis the Hystory and Croniklis of Scotland* (Edinburgh, c. 1540)
H.33.b.7

KING IAMES THE FYFT YE FLOVR OF FLOVRIS
ALL Ў EVER VES IN SCOTLAND OR BE SCHALL HIS
HONOVR MANHEID AND VISDOME TO AVANCE
PAST IN YE ROYAL AND NOBILL REALME OF FRANS
MARIIT YE KINGIS ELDEST DOCHTER SCHEN
QVHA NEMIT VES THE PLESAND MAGDALENE
AND DEIT IN N HIS PALICE CALLIT HALYRVD HOVS

2.3 Kingis and quenis

THE FORMAN ARMORIAL, a collection of arms compiled by Sir Robert Forman of Luthrie, Lord Lyon King of Arms, about 1562 for presentation to Mary, Queen of Scots, is one of several important heraldic compilations of the sixteenth century. It was acquired probably in 1723. Scottish heraldry is a particularly well-developed science. The Lindsay Armorial in the Library's collections (Adv. MS. 31.4.3) is slightly older and, though compiled as a private document by Forman's predecessor as Lyon, Sir David Lindsay of the Mount, was declared in 1630 to be an official record. Another great collection of armorial bearings is the slightly later Seton Armorial (Acc. 9309).

Of the three, the Forman book has a particular charm. This is in part due to the delightful naivety of its representations of the arms of the Scottish peerage and gentry. A special feature of the armorial is the series of paintings of the sovereigns of Scotland and their consorts. The kings wear tabards bearing the royal arms. Their wives display their own armorial bearings (or rather their paternal ones) upon their skirts. King James V and his first queen, Madeleine of France, are thus clearly identifiable here. The ladies carry thistles in vases, as if to show their new identity as queens of Scotland.

Adv. MS. 31.4.2

2.4 Clan, tartan, name and territory

IN THE POPULAR MIND the clan, with its tartan, badges and insignia, is the essence of Scotland, symbolic of family and territorial affiliation. Some of this is genuine and ancient, some merely wished-for and invented. The early Victorian period saw a flowering of research into tartan, clan history and tradition. Some important and magnificent books resulted, of which the finest was *The Clans of the Highlands*. The coloured plates, much celebrated at the time and subsequently much diminished in the form of dinner place-mats, were the work of Robert McIan. The text and commentary ('Descriptions and Historical Memoranda of Character, Mode of Life, etc., etc.') was by James Logan, the pre-eminent contemporary authority on matters Gaelic and 'Highland'. The publisher dedicated the massive two-volume work to the queen, 'who has graciously deigned to visit the Country of the Clans' and who had 'patronised their Manufactures of Costume'. Deigning to visit soon became a royal love-affair with Scotland, leading to the 'Balmorality' of 'Our Life in the Highlands'. The frontispieces of each volume display national emblems surrounded by artistically arranged patterns of the arms of clan chiefs, all set in and on 'frames' of appropriate vegetation.

The Clans of the Highlands. Illustrated by Appropriate Figures Displaying their Dress, Tartans, Arms, Armorial Insignia and Social Occupations, 2 vols (London, 1845)
EL.4.80.11

2.5 The Scottish Parliament before the Union

IN THE 1630s a great hall, with magnificent hammer-beam roof, was built for the use of the unicameral Parliament of Scotland. Here that body sat, until it dissolved itself in 1707, on its incorporation with the Parliament of England in the new Parliament of Great Britain. A lower, or Laigh, Parliament Hall was where the Advocates' Library was accommodated from 1702. The upper Parliament Hall witnessed an historic ceremony in 2004, when members of the new Scottish Parliament, established in 1999, gathered there before moving down the Royal Mile to occupy the new Parliament building at Holyrood. This almost re-created, but in reverse, the ancient 'Riding' or opening of Parliament. The Riding was a procession up the Mile of the three Estates of Parliament to the assembly presided over by the Lord Chancellor of Scotland, and by a Lord High Commissioner representing the monarch absent in London. The

ceremony is shown in this plate, which also affords the only known illustration – although not a very accurate one, particularly from an architectural point of view – of the pre-1707 Parliament in session. The riders have dismounted to process, accompanied by heralds and officials, into the hall. The Library holds a fine set of drawings of the Riding of 1685 (Adv. MS. 31.4.22). These were made, after earlier drawings, by Roderick Chalmers in the 1720s, with one being a still later replacement drawing by none other than Horace Walpole. Two sets of engravings were subsequently made about 1770, and these are also in the collections.

[HENRI] CHATELAIN AND N[ICOLAS] GUEUDEVILLE, *Atlas Historique, ou Nouvelle Introduction à l'Histoire, à la Chronologie & à la Géographie Ancienne & Moderne...*, 7 vols, (Amsterdam, 1720)

E.79.a.11

2.6 A Union book-binding

ELKANAH SETTLE, the author of *Carmen Irenicum* (a poem which occupies 47 pages of turgid verse in Latin and English) may have had this copy bound for some special purpose, possibly royal presentation. The binding is deeply symbolic. The emblems of England and Scotland are entwined, as are the mottoes of the two national orders of chivalry. The rose stem sprouts thistles; the thistle stem roses. The motto of the Order of the Garter spirals upwards to meet the thistle flower, that of the Order of the Thistle to meet the rose bloom. Beneath a royal crown, the national emblems are conjoined by a Garter Star; below that is a dove of peace. At great length the poem, dedicated to Queen Anne, lauds (as its preface expresses it) 'so Universal a Blessing, the Union of Two (now truly happy) Kingdoms', a 'shining Labour' safely accomplished. Settle barely presumes to imagine the 'Transports of Delight' with which the sovereign, of a 'now United-Britain', contemplates her great work in private: 'we must intrude even into Her Retiring Closet for so Sublime a Speculation: For Her Raptures are only rais'd highest, when Her Knee bends lowest.' To the 'Patriots of Great Britain' he addresses these words: '… from this dazzling Review of the warm Zeal within your *Senatory-Walls* in that Illustrious Cause…You have rendered Yourselves, a new United-Nation, too Formidable, to fear the starting up of any new Insults from

irregular Ambition to disturb the future Repose of the World.' London ('Augusta') 'Bows to salute, no more an *Alien* now, / Her darling inmate Sister *Edinbro*.'

ELKANAH SETTLE, *Carmen Irenicum. The Union of the Imperial Crowns of Great Britain. An Heroick Poem* (London, 1707)
F.5.c.16

2.7
The Adam brothers' British order

BY THE 1770S, when the architect brothers Robert and James Adam published this design (the conception of it was largely James's), the Union was secure after three abortive risings in favour of the exiled Stuart dynasty. The Hanoverian throne was unassailable. Britain had emerged from the Seven Years' War as a truly world power. She was fast becoming the greatest industrial economy, and a leader in science and the arts. Peace and prosperity reigned at home. The Adams, Edinburgh architects and designers who had left Scotland ('a narrow place', Robert Adam called it) to make their fame and fortune in London, dreamed of even greater things: prestigious public commissions for royal and government buildings in the capital. The dilettante James Adam designed this order for a gateway at Carlton House, more by way of advertisement than in any serious hope of ever building such a structure. It is the Union expressed in stone and stucco. Probably only a Scottish architect could have conceived and drawn it; an Englishman had no need to make such an obvious statement of loyalty to the United Kingdom. Lions and unicorns (English and Scottish heraldic supporters) frolic amid classical acanthus *rinceaux*. The abacus of the capital is adorned with a moulding of alternating acorns and pine-cones above the collar of the Garter. The volutes are composed of more lions and unicorns leaping from acanthus interwoven with roses and thistles.

The Works in Architecture of Robert and James Adam, Esquires vol. 1, part V, Designs for the King and Queen and HRH the late Princess Dowager of Wales (London, 1778)
L.C. Fol.1

2.8 George IV in Edinburgh, 1822

THE NATIONAL LIBRARY's principal building is on Edinburgh's George IV Bridge. The street name recalls the celebrated visit made by the king in August 1822, the first to Scotland by a reigning monarch for almost 200 years. It is impossible to overstate the importance of this occasion. Conceived and stage-managed in every detail by Sir Walter Scott, this was an event designed to do many things: to reconcile past and present, Jacobite ghosts with Hanoverian realities, Highland tradition and Lowland progress; to make the kilt and the broadsword acceptable to a capital city, and a monarchy perceived as English, which had not so long before stood in fear of them; and so on. The 'King's Jaunt' was one of the key events of Georgian Scotland. Scott had earlier searched for, and brought to light, the Honours of Scotland, the crown and regalia laid up in Edinburgh Castle after the Union of 1707 and subsequently forgotten. A central feature of the visit of 1822 was the presentation to the king of these traditional symbols of Scottish sovereignty, nationhood and independence. Robert Mudie published a detailed account of the ceremony and proceedings, illustrated with several folding plates of highlights of the visit. Here the king is seen arriving in state at Edinburgh Castle, there to ascend the ramparts and acknowledge the salute of the people. This ceremony, and its location on the castle esplanade, together give a foretaste of the world-famous military tattoo which was first held on this spot in 1950 and has since become a high point of the Scottish tourist year. Modern Tattoo audiences are seated in stands not so very dissimilar from those of 1822, though Scott and his friends clearly recognised something about the Edinburgh weather that escaped the notice or the capabilities of later organisers: these stands are roofed.

[ROBERT MUDIE], *A Historical Account of His Majesty's Visit to Scotland* (Edinburgh, 1822)

F.5.f.16

2.9 Bound for the law

BOOKBINDING IS ONE of the minor arts of eighteenth-century Scotland in which real distinction, worthy of international attention, was achieved. James and William Scott were the particular masters of the craft, working in a distinctive classical style that was somewhere between the baroque and the neoclassical, and which on occasion seems almost to reflect the wall-decoration of Herculaneum and Pompeii. But there were many other distinguished binders, working earlier or later than the Scotts, most of them anonymous. The most prevalent styles were based upon the motifs known as the 'herring-bone' and the 'wheel'. These, with the 'central lozenge' design, predominate in a specialist, but interesting and attractive, class of bindings: those applied to the slim

theses, written in Latin on some discrete aspect of the 'Pandects' or civil law, by 'intrants' to the Faculty of Advocates as the final part of their 'trials' for admission to the Bar. These were often dedicated to senior counsel or judges. The young man whose thesis is illustrated above right, William Adam, later became the most distinguished of the group, as Lord Chief Commissioner of the Jury Court. His, in fact the earliest in date, was also perhaps the most splendid as a work of art, with its coruscating *rayonné* wheel-spokes. But taste and design were in his blood: he was the son of John Adam, eldest of the Adam brothers, and his uncles, Robert and James, might have taken a more than passing interest in the elegance of the design.

Bdg.s.23, Bdg.s.30, Bdg.s.31

2.10 Scott for the defence

IN 1800 ONE GEORGE ELLIOT, horse-dealer in Hawick, was indicted on a charge of issuing forged guinea banknotes. His counsel at his trial in the High Court of Justiciary, sitting in Edinburgh, was Walter Scott. Scott, already appointed Sheriff-Depute of Selkirkshire, a published author of translations from German literature and ever more engrossed in the business of ballad hunting, collecting and editing, was evidently at this stage still willing and able to practise, on occasion, as an advocate. He prepared a long and eloquent defence for Elliot: it was printed in full and extends to 43 pages. This, and other legal papers connected with the case, were bound up and came to form part of the Abbotsford Collection, bought from Major-General Sir Walter Maxwell-Scott in 1934. The printed papers are followed by some sheets of Scott's manuscript notes. The final page, with its doodled drawing of Scott's unfortunate client being hanged, offers his in-court view of how the trial might go – testimony to his opinion as to his client's likely fate, and perhaps of Scott's lack of confidence in his own advocacy.

MS. 1628

2.11 An advocate in court

ONE OF THE GREATEST pleaders of his day, John Clerk was the son of John Clerk of Eldin, the etcher, geologist and naval tactician (cf. 1.4 and 4.11). Eccentric, coarse-mannered, rough-spoken and more than combative, the younger Clerk was born for the cut-and-thrust of legal action, both civil and criminal. He defended Deacon William Brodie, the infamous housebreaker. He liked nothing more than to outwit judges, even taking on, and humiliating, the Lord Chancellor when pleading in the House of Lords. He himself rose to be a senator of the College of Justice, as Lord Eldin, but the bench did not suit his fiery temperament. He was also a man of taste, however, and his picture collection was one of the greatest non-aristocratic ones ever assembled in Scotland. Clerk was the subject of a fine portrait by his friend Henry Raeburn, showing him as the connoisseur; but this watercolour by John Gibson Lockhart, a junior fellow advocate, who wrote of Clerk memorably in the brilliant *Peter's Letters to his Kinsfolk*, catches him in full oratorical flood in the courtroom that was his natural element. Walter Scott, Lockhart's father-in-law, said of the artist that he had a 'pretty talent' for caricature. But Lockhart was noted for a biting wit even more mordant than the acid with which this image was later etched (there are two versions in Acc. 11480), and was known in the *Blackwood's Magazine* circle of writers as 'The Scorpion'.

MS. 1626, f. 70

Faith and Religion 3

3.1 Piety warmer in Iona

WRITTEN AND ILLUMINATED probably in or near Oxford between 1180 and 1220, the manuscript book known as the Iona Psalter was made for a nun in a Scottish Augustinian house. She was perhaps Beatrix, first prioress of Iona, daughter of Somerled, Lord of the Isles. A kalendar of saints associated with Iona is included. Medieval liturgical books made for Scottish owners are rare and often of indifferent quality, but Oxford was a great centre of book production, and the status of the likely owner ensured a level of patronage allowing exceptional work to be commissioned. Both script and decoration are done to a very high standard.

The remarkable artistry combines different traditions of illumination, with large historiated (that is, 'inhabited' or 'story-telling') initial letters, spiralling Celtic-style decoration, and charming beasts, fishes and human heads employed as fillers at the end of lines. From the later eighteenth century Iona, as a centre of early Scottish Christianity, was a much visited and venerated spot for tourists and pilgrims. Samuel Johnson captured the special magic of the island when he wrote: 'That man is little to be envied… whose piety would not grow warmer among the ruins of Iona.'
MS. 10,000

3.2 Not *that* Blackadder...

THIS PRAYERBOOK WAS probably once owned by Robert Blackadder, archbishop of Glasgow, 1483-1508. A particularly intriguing and attractive manuscript, it is thought to have been written and illuminated in France. Scholars are interested in questions of provenance, and this is a book rich in evidence of previous ownership. In-text allusion and illustration points to Blackadder; a later archbishop of St Andrews is mentioned on the flyleaf; and the fine Parisian binding of yet later date points to another Scottish owner, Alexander, fifth Lord Livingston. The volume is something of a hybrid: neither really a psalter, nor yet strictly a book of hours, it contains additional prayers and Gospel passages as well as the usual liturgical components making up the standard book of hours. It is richly supplied with a fine series of illuminated miniature paintings and initial letters, including images of the Scottish saints Ninian and Margaret. It is tempting to think that one of the largest miniatures (illustrated here), showing a kneeling cleric in prayer before the crucified Christ in a landscape beside a church, is in fact intended to represent Archbishop Blackadder himself. If so, it would parallel the image of James Brown, dean of Aberdeen, in his prayerbook of similar date, also in the Library (MS. 10270). Images such as these are statements of personal piety and devotion, much as the Flemish altarpieces which include the donor or others at prayer.

MS. 10271

A paradoxical message in a binding

THIS SPLENDID BINDING by James Scott adorns a copy, intended for presentation to King George III, of *Scotland's Opposition to the Popish Bill* (Edinburgh 1780), a collection of declarations and resolutions from all over Scotland against repeal of anti-Catholic legislation. The man who may have commissioned this binding, and who was certainly intimately connected with its production, was Lord George Gordon, eccentric (or mentally unstable) son of the third Duke of Gordon, and begetter of the infamous London riots of 1780 that bear his name. Gordon led the Protestant Association opposed to the toleration and relief of Catholics. He seems to have believed that his cause would be furthered by presentation to the king and the prince of Wales of this monotonous assemblage of expressions of intolerance. After his acquittal on a charge of high treason, Gordon attempted to give the book to the sovereign at a *levée* in 1781 – an exasperated Lord North, the prime minister, having suggested that this was the way to get his message across. King George refused to accept the book. It would be hard to find a binding more inappropriate to its purpose. It looks strongly 'papist', with its emblematic risen Christ in the centre, and is highly charged with symbolism suggestive of Rome: trophies of arms, classical heads within laurel wreaths, trumpeting seraphim, garlands and swags, but with some token thistles added for good (or bad) measure.
Ry. II.e.49

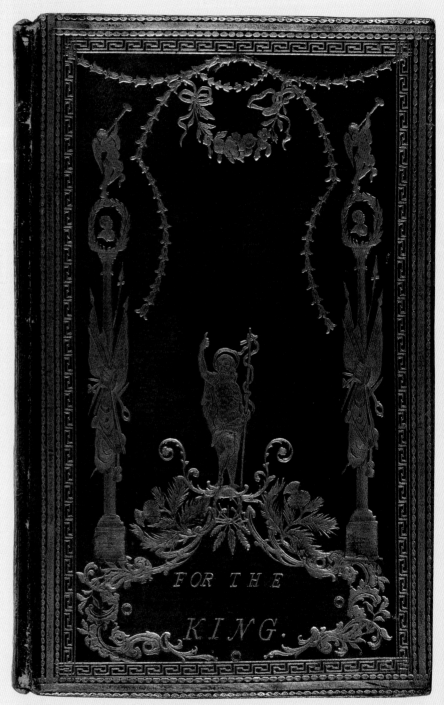

3.4 The ark of Ardnamurchan

AFTER MANY YEARS of debate on matters of lay patronage which had divided parishioners and clergy throughout the country, the Disruption of 1843 split Presbyterian Scotland between the existing Church of Scotland and a new Free Church. The result of this cataclysmic secession was that many ministers lost their livings and were turned out not only of their churches, but their manses too, since the great majority of those landowners who were not Episcopalian were adherents of the established church. Large areas, particularly in the remote western Highlands and Islands, were left without places of worship or adequate provision of clergy for the spiritual needs of Free Church adherents. Landowners exercised their rights by refusing sites for Free Church building. The new denomination looked seaward for salvation. First, a yacht was commissioned to take ministers to far-flung communicants. For ten years this vessel served a sea-girt flock. Then, in 1845, the Free Church ordered a floating iron

church from a Port Glasgow shipyard. It was towed to its anchorage off Strontian in Loch Sunart. An indifferent but intriguing image shows this spiritual leviathan, which could accommodate between 750 and 1000 worshippers. The congregation was rowed out in boats in a time-consuming and uncomfortable process of embarkation and disembarkation, and a gauge indicating how the vessel sat in the water measured the numbers on board. It must have resembled a giant shed or hangar: one adherent, however, likened it improbably to 'one of the neater churches of the metropolis'. In the US at almost the same time floating churches for seamen might be seen in the East River, off New York City, and in the Delaware, off Philadelphia, though these (unlike their Scottish poor relation) were palpably, if vicariously, Puginesque. The man who conceived the iron church, Sheriff Graham Speirs, wrote of it as 'this ark, for the preservation of His own Word among our distant congregations … on the bosom of the deep, until the waters of bitterness have subsided'.

THOMAS BROWN, *Annals of the Disruption...1843* (Edinburgh, 1893)
ABS.3.80.7

3.5 Moses in a top hat

IN 1856 AN EDINBURGH uncle offered a prize to his nephews and his own children for the best history of Moses. His family was the Stevensons, and the winner of the competition was the six-year old Robert Louis Balfour Stevenson. The story Louis composed – he was allowed to dictate it to his mother, in whose hand it survives – was the product of five successive Sunday evenings before Christmas. The manuscript, extending to 23 pages of Mrs Stevenson's writing and signed at the end by her son, is not RLS's earliest known holograph, but it is indeed the first work of his genius and imagination. The manuscript is accompanied by a series of delightful drawings by the young 'author' himself: to the

naivety of these is added the charm of the characters' appearance, for these Israelites wear stove-pipe or 'lum' (as they were known in Scotland) hats and smoke pipes and cigars. On occasion a camel incongruously appears beside the citizens of Auld Reekie, and Moses (in a tail coat) sits to write his tablets on a chair that comes straight from an Edinburgh New Town drawing-room. Preserved with the original *Stevensoniana* is the copy of *The Happy Sunday Book of Painted Pictures*, inscribed to him by his uncle, which was RLS's juvenile prize. From this moment, Stevenson's mother recorded, 'it was the desire of his heart to be an author'. The 'History of Moses' manuscript and group of drawings was formerly in several US collections, and was bought by the Library in 1991.

Acc. 10356

3.6 An ox-wagon pulpit

Scottish enterprise in the mission field was as great as that in any other area of overseas endeavour, though it lacked the glamour of soldiering, the worldly success of imperial administration, or the wealth that was to be acquired (sometimes questionably) by mercantile activity or plantation owning. The Library is particularly rich in holdings relating to the activities of the Scots missions: it holds the official archives and records of the all the various Scottish Presbyterian churches active in the mission field over the century between 1827 and 1929, and in every part of the world to which Scotland sent its missionary sons and daughters. The African dimension to this activity is particularly important, and here the official records complement the papers, diaries and correspondence of individual missionaries and explorers, most notably David Livingstone, the first of whose papers were acquired in 1937. The Library is now the word's leading centre for Livingstone research. Livingstone's father-in-law was Robert Moffat, a native of Ormiston, East Lothian, who joined the London Missionary Society and served in South Africa between 1816 and 1870 with only one break. Moffat's *Missionary Labours* bears upon its title-page a vignette which illustrates an experience of preaching in Bechuanaland on the edge of the Kalahari desert. Moffat described the episode: 'I was astonished to find a congregation waiting before the wagon… I confess I was more inclined to take a cup of coffee than to preach a sermon… taking the text "God so loved the world" [I] discoursed to them for about an hour. Great order and profound silence were maintained… The earnest attention manifested exceeded any thing I had ever before witnessed, and the countenances of some indicated strong mental excitement.' The missionary's lot could be a happy one.

Robert Moffat, *Missionary Labours and Scenes in Southern Africa* (London, 1842)

E.151.e.15

3.7 Not quite eaten: tartan protects

The lion, rather than the proverbial cannibal, was more likely to threaten the life of a missionary. David Livingstone recounted his narrow escape from the jaws of one beast. 'Growling horribly close to my ear, he shook me as a terrier dog does a rat. The shock produced a stupor similar to that which seems to be felt by a mouse after the first shake of the cat. It caused a sort of dreaminess, in which there was no sense of pain nor feeling of terror… It was like what patients partially under the influence of chloroform describe, who see all the operation but feel not the knife…' The lion, already shot by Livingstone, was drawn off by his companions, both of whom were bitten. The animal succumbed to the gunshot wounds. The missionary's injury proved less damaging, long-term, than those sustained by his African retainers. A strange Scottish reason was advanced for this, and somehow one is transported to a world of the 'Garb of Old Gaul' and heraldic beasts. 'I had on a tartan jacket', Livingstone wrote, 'and I believe that it wiped off all the virus from the teeth that pierced the flesh, for my two companions in this affray have both suffered from the peculiar pains, while I have escaped with only the inconvenience of a false joint in my limb.' The engraving by J.W. Whymper (aptly named) shows the lion *passant* rather than *rampant* over the tartan-clad missionary. Livingstone's trademark cap lies beside him.

David Livingstone, *Missionary Travels and Researches in South Africa* (London, 1857)

RB.s.972

Konzentrationslager Auschwitz

Folgende Anordnungen sind beim Schriftverkehr mit Häftlingen zu beachten:

1. Jeder Schutzhäftling darf im Monat zwei Briefe oder zwei Karten von seinen Angehörigen empfangen und an sie absenden. Briefe an die Häftlinge müssen lesbar mit Tinte, einseitig und in deutscher Sprache geschrieben sein. Gestattet sind nur Briefbogen in normaler Größe. Briefumschläge ungefüttert. Einem Briefe dürfen nur 5 Briefmarken à 12 Pf. der Deutschen Reichspost beigelegt werden. Alles andere ist verboten und unterliegt der Beschlagnahme. Lichtbilder dürfen als Postkarten nich' verwendet werden.

2. Geldsendungen sind nur durch Postanweisungen gestattet. Es ist darauf zu achten, daß bei Geld- oder Postsendungen die genaue Anschrift, bestehend aus Name, Geburtsdatum und Nr. angegeben ist. Bei fehlerhaften Anschriften geht die Post an den Absender zurück oder wird vernichtet.

3. Zeitungen sind gestattet, dürfen aber nur durch die Poststelle des K.L. Auschwitz bestellt werden.

4. Die Häftlinge dürfen Lebensmittelpakete empfangen, Flüssigkeiten und Medikamente sind jedoch nicht gestattet.

5. Gesuche an die Lagerleitung zwecks Entlassung aus der Schutzhaft sind zwecklos.

6. Sprecherlaubnis und Besuche von Häftlingen im Lager sind grundsätzlich nicht gestattet.

Der Lagerkommandant.

3.8 'Arbeit macht frei'

JANE HAINING, from Dunscore in Dumfriesshire, had gone to Hungary in 1932. There she served as matron of the Church of Scotland's Jewish mission committee Budapest Girls' Home (the Budapest mission had been established as long ago as 1841.) She took the city and its Jewish community to her heart; a visiting Church of Scotland minister described her as 'a fine example of the Scot abroad – the most Scottish thing in the Scottish mission, with her sonsy face and cheery smile and unmistakable accent'. Having come home on leave in the summer of 1939, she elected to go back to Budapest in September, soon to be cut off from Scotland and forced to remain there for the duration of the war. Refusing to leave her children, she declined instructions from the missionary committee to try to extricate herself by way of Istanbul and Palestine. Instead, in March 1944, she was obliged to sew with her own hands a yellow Star of David to the clothing of each of her charges. Arrested by the Gestapo, she was imprisoned and transferred to Auschwitz, where she died in July 1944. The letter shown was written (in German) two days before her death. Its survival is remarkable, but it seems even stranger to learn that she was permitted to send an ordinary letter to the outside world. Postmark and stamp are chilling. In March 2010, Jane Haining was among the first recipients of the new Heroes of the Holocaust award.

From the papers of the Foreign, Jewish, Colonial and Continental Mission Committees of the Church of Scotland

Acc. 7548, G.46a

War and Conflict 4

4.1 **Highland intrepidity**

IN THE FRENCH REVOLUTIONARY and Napoleonic wars, Scottish regiments greatly distinguished themselves in every theatre of a truly world conflict. The fighting Scotsman was a familiar sight to inspire confidence in his fellow British soldiers and terror in the enemy. Even before this time, the government had seen the sense of allowing Scottish soldiers to wear once again the traditional Highland habit, generally proscribed for some years after Culloden as symbolic of a feared and hated opponent. The kilt, plaid, feather bonnet and broadsword, and the varied tartans and accoutrements of the newly raised Highland regiments, were now to be seen on the battlefields of India, Egypt, Sicily, Portugal, Spain, Holland, France and Belgium. After the fall of Napoleon, kilted Scottish troops fascinated the women of Paris, who were frequently seen in cartoons bent-double and trying to satisfy themselves as to the age-old question! Rowlandson's fine book of plates, done in co-operation with the Angelo fencing-masters, was actually a manual of arms and sword-exercises for the Light Horse Volunteers of London and Westminster. But, for some reason, possibly the sheer glamour of the Highland soldier, Rowlandson included two plates showing a Highland officer engaging a French opponent and wounding him through agility and intelligent sword-play.

Hungarian & Highland Broad Sword. Twenty Four Plates designed and etched by T. Rowlandson, under the direction of Messrs H. Angelo and Son... (London, 1799)

FB.l.136

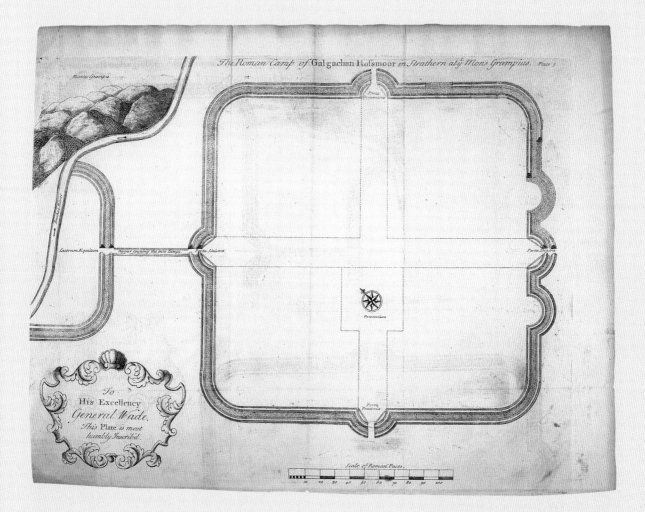

The Roman Camp of Galgachan Ho∫smoor *in Strathern al∫ Mons Grampius.* Plate 5

To
His Excellency
General Wade,
This Plate is most
humbly Inscrib'd

Scale of Roman Paces.

4.2 'In the garb of old Gaul with the fire of old Rome'

TACITUS TELLS US that in AD83 or 84 the Roman general Agricola fought the battle of Mons Graupius against Caledonian tribes led by Calgacus. The speech that the historian put into Calgacus's mouth was used seventeen centuries later by nationalist historians and antiquaries for a variety of purposes. Alexander Gordon is a striking example. He delighted in the sentimental idea that ancient Caledonia had resisted, and ultimately thrown off, the Roman yoke. He translated this idea into his own time, in his wish that Scots living in a post-Union world might resist English domination in fields ranging from economics to culture, or even outdo those whom he regarded as playing a 'Roman' role in the Scotland of his day. Gordon appeared to accept the speech of Calgacus as reportage by, rather than artifice on the part of, Tacitus: it contained 'such a Strain of Patriotism and Love of

Liberty… that there is not such a glorious Piece of Eloquence committed to the Roman Language'. He was led to search for Roman camps, forts and battlefields on the strength of this. Illustrated here is what he thought were the remains of Agricola's camp before Mons Graupius, near Comrie in Strathearn: 'in all my Travels through Britain, I never beheld any Thing with more Pleasure, it being directly at the Foot of the *Grampian Hills*… In fine, to an Antiquary, this is a ravishing Scene.' Paradoxically Gordon dedicated this plate to General George Wade, overlooking the fact that the English soldier had just completed an exercise in 'bridling the Highlands' with roads and barracks – just like a Roman.
ALEXANDER GORDON, *Itinerarium Septentrionale: or, a Journey thro' most of the Counties of Scotland...* (London, 1726)
L.C. 1247

4.3 Braveheart

THE MANUSCRIPTS OF Henry (Blind Harry) the Minstrel's
'Wallace' and John Barbour's 'The Bruce' (Adv. MSS 19.2.2, i
and ii) are primary sources for the lives of the two great Scottish
patriots of fact and legend. In popular culture, however, the film
version, *Braveheart*, assumes priority. Somewhere in between
the two is the novel *The Scottish Chiefs*, first published in 1810,
which enjoyed enormous and enduring success and was widely
translated. Its author, Jane Porter, grew up and was educated
in Edinburgh, and her historical fiction actually anticipated
Walter Scott's. *The Scottish Chiefs* takes Wallace for its hero.
One of the finest editions is that published by Charles Scribner's
Sons of New York (and in Britain by Hodder and Stoughton)
in 1921. The illustrations by N.C. Wyeth, perhaps the greatest
American book-illustrator of the day, are striking, even if they
lack strict historical verisimilitude. 'The Pledge' is pure 'Braveheart' *avant la lettre*, but with no apparent face-painting.

JANE PORTER, *The Scottish Chiefs*, edited by Kate Douglas Wiggin and
Nora A. Smith; illustrated by N.C. Wyeth (New York and London, 1921)
X.201.f

4.4 Flodden's fatal field

DESCRIBED AS THE earliest known English news pamphlet,
...*The Trewe Encountre*... was published in London in 1513.
It is an eyewitness account of the famous engagement in
September that year at Branxton Moor, Northumberland,
the largest battle ever fought between the 'auld enemies',
Scotland and England. This eight-page publication stands at
the head of the long tradition of British journalism, and is the
precursor of the newspapers of today. Copies of the original
pamphlet are very rare. The Library does not have one; but it
does have a copy of the reprint, on vellum, of 1809, produced
'under the revise of Mr [Joseph] Haslewood'. The huge
popularity of Walter Scott's *Marmion: a tale of Flodden Field*,
published the previous year, was one possible reason for the
reprint of this old pamphlet about the battle. Capitalising in a
similar way on the success of Scott's poem, the amateur artist
Sir James Stuart, would later (1821) publish an album of
Illustrations to Scott and Byron (ABS.8.78.3) which contains
some spirited images inspired by *Marmion*. *The Trewe
Encountre* has an illustration showing the crown of the fallen
king of Scots, James IV, being brought to the pavilion of the
victorious commander. An English 'honours list', as in *The
London Gazette*, brings up the rear. A Scottish 'casualty list' is
included: truly were 'The Flowers of the Forest all wede away'.

...*The Trewe Encountre, or Batayle lately don betwene Englande and
Scotlande*...(London, 1809)
RB. s. 1933

4.5

'And we ran, and they ran...'

The battle of Sheriffmuir effectively ended the 1715 Jacobite rebellion, but its inconclusive nature, and the partiality of both sides in claiming victory, led to much subsequent satirical writing about the action. Robert Burns followed in a long tradition when he wrote 'Sherra-Moor' for *The Scots Musical Museum* in 1790; it furnishes an interesting example of Burns as commentator on long-past historical events. He bases his poem on older verse accounts, showing his ability and willingness to 'improve' upon existing songs and ballads, while making them distinctively his own. Two shepherds discuss their differing interpretations of the action: one suggests that the Hanoverian government commander, the Duke of Argyll, had trounced the Jacobite Earl of Mar. The other says the very reverse happened. Both can verify it. An etching by David Allan catches the spirit of the indecisive battle, and its record in verse. Interestingly, Allan has dressed his fleeing figures (Highland Jacobite, and Lowland or government) in the uniform of his own time, the 1780s and 1790s, rather than in that of 1715. The manuscript was bought by the Library in 2009 to mark the 250th anniversary of the poet's birth.

Acc. 13039

Sangs of the Lowlands of Scotland (Edinburgh 1798)

NG.1168.a.21

C v 2 fo 282

O cam ye here the fight to shun,
Or herd the sheep wi' me, man;
Or ware ye at the Sherra-muir,
And did the battle see, man?
I saw the battle sair and tough, (and reekin-red ran mony a sheugh)
My heart for fear gae sough for sough,
To hear the thuds, and see the cluds
O' Clans frae woods, in tartan duds,
~~O' Clans frae woods, in tartan duds,~~
Wha glaum'd at kingdoms three, man.

The red-coat lads wi' black cockades
To meet them were na slaw, man;
They rush'd, and push'd, and blude outgush'd,
And mony a bouk did fa', man:
The great Argyle led on his files,
they glanced twenty miles, though the Clans like nine-pin kyles
They hack'd and hash'd, while broadswords clash'd,
And thro' they dash'd, and hew'd and smash'd,
~~And thro' they~~ &c.
Till fey men dy'd awa, man.

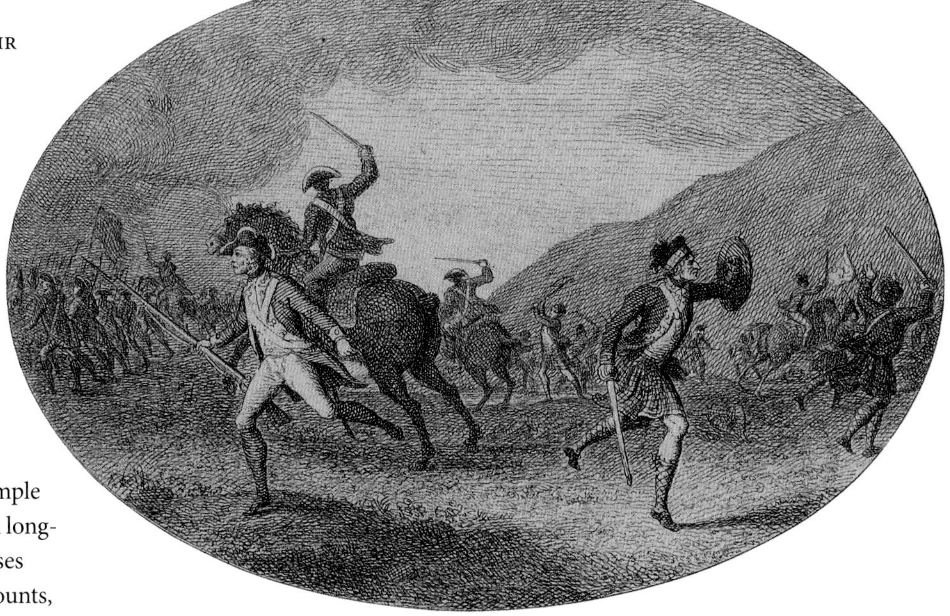

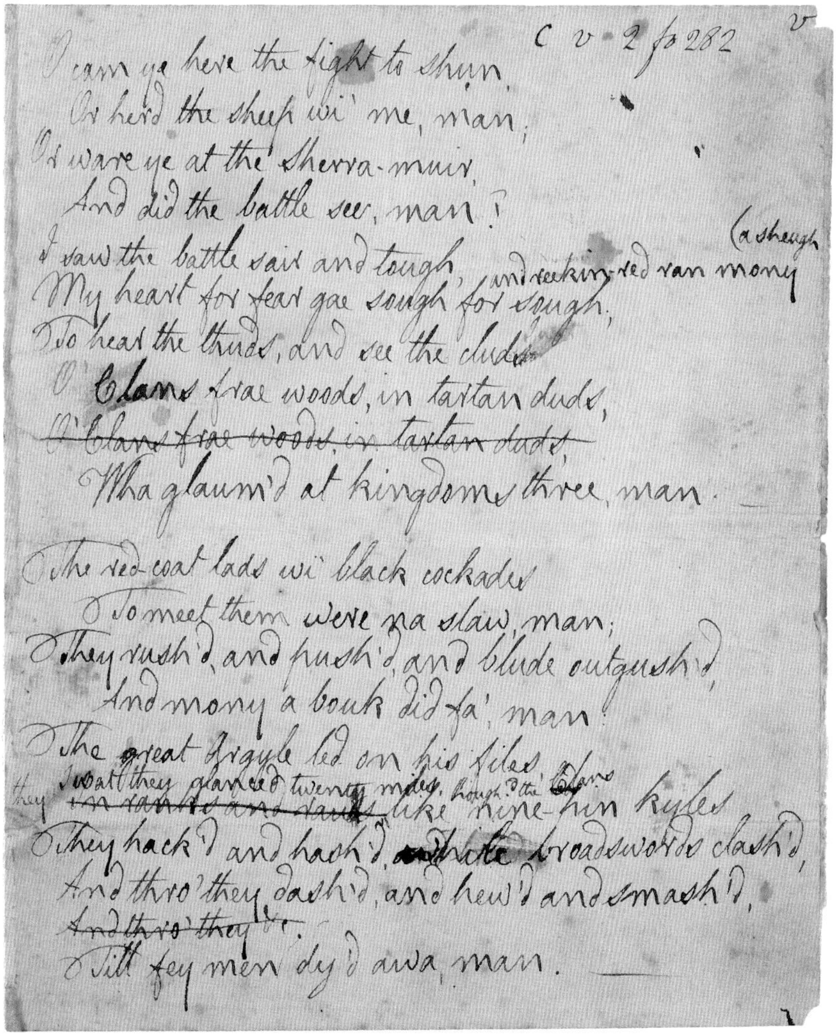

4.6 The hero and the coward

THESE ETCHINGS BY David Allan have been overlooked by those searching for imagery of the Jacobite rebellion of 1745. The battle of Prestonpans, or Tranent-Muir, was the rebellion's greatest success; it terrified the Lowland Whigs, and shook the British government in London. Sir John Cope became a byword for military incompetence, before and during the battle, and for cowardice immediately afterwards. The judgment of contemporaries was somewhat too harsh, and that of posterity rather unjust: and the Library's recent acquisition (Acc. 11771) of the papers Cope assembled for his defence at the board of enquiry into his conduct (it was not a court martial) are an important source for military historians. Allan shows Bonnie Prince Charlie as the dashing glamour-boy hero of the hour, Cope as the corpulent Hanoverian officer in flight towards Berwick, ignorant of and uncaring for the whereabouts and state of his broken troops. The splendid song 'Hey, Johnny Cope' was written by Adam Skirving, who also composed 'Tranent-Muir', which Allan illustrates. The viewer should not be misled by the word 'Cillicrankie': this traditional tune, to which is set the verses on Prestonpans, here illustrated by Allan (below), refers to the earlier Jacobite victory by James Graham of Claverhouse ('Bonnie Dundee') at Killiecrankie in 1689.

From the album entitled in manuscript 'Etchings from Scottish Songs by D. Allan for G. Thomson'

FB.s.383

4.7 A gamble lost

A MORE MOVING relic of the 1745 rebellion could hardly be imagined than this account of the battle of Culloden and its aftermath of pursuit and harsh reprisal. Captain Felix O'Neil was an Irish officer in attendance on Prince Charles Edward. During the flight of 'the Prince in the Heather' after the defeat of his army, O'Neil (we may imagine) lay up for a time, and wrote his account on all that he happened to have in his pocket at the time – a pack of playing-cards. Bishop Robert Forbes included this text in his compilation of Jacobite materials, which concentrates on the dangers and sufferings of the hunted, the dispossessed and the attainted after Culloden and the failure of the rising. This, 'The Lyon in Mourning', is another Jacobite manuscript treasure in the Library's collections (Adv. MS. 32.6.18-26).

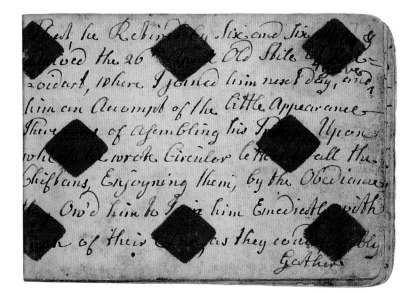

Forbes, bishop of Ross and Caithness, had been arrested on suspicion before he could join the rising, as he had intended. Perhaps as a sort of compensation for his forced inactivity in this time of crisis, he devoted many subsequent years to the compilation of his invaluable collection of source materials, afterwards long concealed since the writing of it was a treasonable offence. His volumes contain even such affecting relics as fragments of Prince Charles's Garter ribbon and sword-hilt lining, and of the dress he wore when disguised as Flora Macdonald's maid 'Betty Burk'.

Acc. 5491

4.8 'Butcher Cumberland'

PRINCE WILLIAM AUGUSTUS, a younger son of King George II, proved to be a capable general and is famous (to some, infamous) as victor of Culloden. His measures to extinguish the last embers of the fire of Jacobitism after the battle were regarded as unnecessarily brutal. The epithet 'Butcher' was apparently coined at a later date when his freemanship of a City of London livery company was mooted: 'Let it be of the Butchers', a wit suggested. Walter Biggar Blaikie, of the great Edinburgh printing house of T. & A. Constable, was an authority on the history of Jacobitism. His collection, donated to the Library in 1928, includes an extensive and important selection of engravings on topics connected with the Stuarts and the several ill-fated risings in their name. The print illustrated here, showing Cumberland flaying an unfortunate Highlander, is entitled: 'This is the Butcher beware of your Sheep'.

Blk. SNPG.1.5

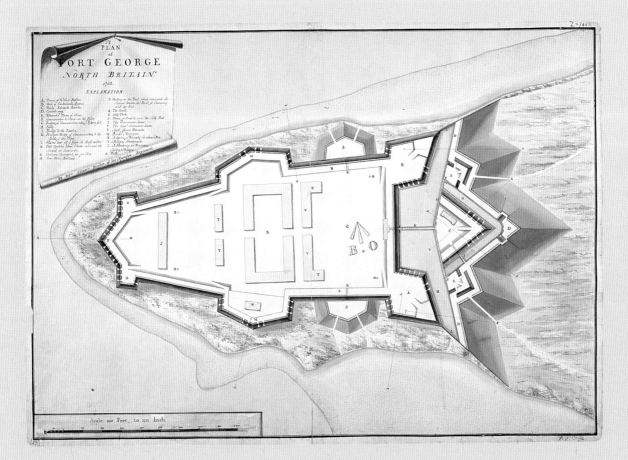

4.9 Never again!

THE BRITISH GOVERNMENT programme to pacify, control and ultimately 'civilise' the northern parts of 'North Britain', so that further pro-Jacobite unrest might not erupt in open rebellion, had begun not long after the Union. The risings of 1715 and 1745 came and went, and Hanoverian power was asserted more forcefully still by the construction of the immensely strong Fort George on a spit of land at Ardersier, near Inverness. This was, by some measure, the most formidable of all the Highland forts, barracks and garrisons which, with their interconnecting roads and bridges begun by General Wade, lay like a weighted net upon some captive beast. The Board of Ordnance Plans (as the very large collection of drawings and maps is known) were deposited in the Library by the War Office in 1934.

The government had by this time realised that the likely threat from the Highlands to the peace and safety of Edinburgh, London, England as a whole, the established church and the monarchy had probably safely passed! This plan of Fort George is one of a comprehensive series for that building alone. The draughtsmanship and artistry of the Board of Ordnance series is very fine: surveyors of the calibre of Paul Sandby were employed. Architects such as William Adam worked as designers and contractors for the government, and his sons John, Robert and James cut their architectural teeth on Ordnance contracting. William Skinner, the military engineer in charge at Fort George, drew this plan with its *trompe l'oeil* cartouche.

MS. 1646, Z02/45a

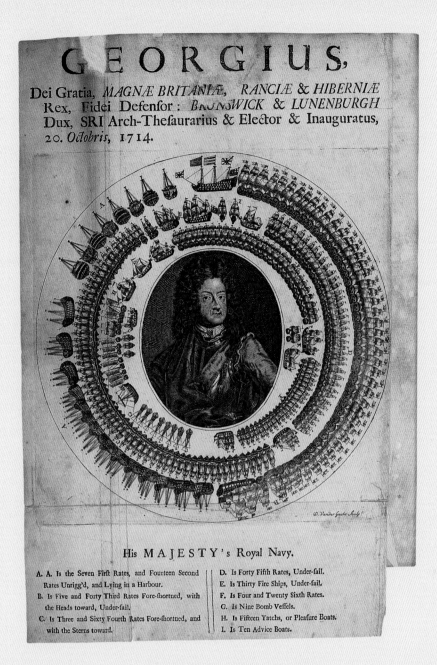

GEORGIUS,

Dei Gratia, *MAGNÆ BRITANIÆ, FRANCIÆ & HIBERNIÆ* Rex, Fidei Defenſor: BRUNSWICK & LUNENBURGH Dux, SRI Arch-Theſaurarius & Elector & Inauguratus, 20. *Octobris*, 1714.

His MAJESTY's Royal Navy.

A. A. Is the Seven Firſt Rates, and Fourteen Second Rates Unrigg'd, and Lying in a Harbour.
B. Is Five and Forty Third Rates Fore-ſhortned, with the Heads toward, Under-ſail.
C. Is Three and Sixty Fourth Rates Fore-ſhortned, and with the Sterns toward.
D. Is Forty Fifth Rates, Under-ſail.
E. Is Thirty Fire Ships, Under-ſail.
F. Is Four and Twenty Sixth Rates.
G. Is Nine Bomb Veſſels.
H. Is Fifteen Yatchs, or Pleaſure Boats.
I. Is Ten Advice Boats.

4.10 The wooden walls of Scotland

AFTER 1707, Scots of all classes found fresh opportunities for advancement in the newly established United Kingdom. Many tempting worlds opened to them, at home and abroad, and the archetype later characterised by James Barrie as 'the Scotsman on the make' began to materialise. The print-sellers' shops soon became full of satirical caricatures of avaricious or needy Scotsmen, descending upon London (sometimes literally, from the sky, borne on kilts like parachutes) in pursuit of fortune, if not always fame. The hugely expanding Royal Navy, with a vast building programme that transformed the economy and agriculture, as well as aspects of the working and social life of Britain, offered many chances: one tends to overlook the fact that so many Scots served in a fleet still largely perceived as 'English', both on the upper and lower decks. William Sutherland's manual of shipbuilding opens with a schematic, extremely effective and impressive view of the enhanced and re-invigorated navy, arranged by rates of vessel, around the portrait of King George I. Scotland's own time as a great shipbuilding nation, exemplified in the word 'Clyde-built', was at this point some way in the future. But it would come.

WILLIAM SUTHERLAND, *Britain's Glory: or, Ship-Building Unveil'd...* (London, 1717)

X.21.a

4.11 How to break the line (but don't tell the French)

THE MULTI-TALENTED John Clerk of Eldin (cf. 1.45) played a major part in the development of the tactics which won the Royal Navy a series of astounding victories, culminating in the annihilation in 1805 of the combined fleets of France and Spain at Trafalgar. Clerk was not himself a sailor, though he had brothers in the navy. Using little cork and wax models, which still survive, he applied his fertile mind to the problems of superiority in action at critical moments, and the tactics of overwhelming part of an enemy's line of battle before the rest of his fleet could turn to assist. Clerk's work evolved though various editions and enlargements of an original publication of 1782. The London edition of

1790 was immediately translated into French and published in Paris in 1791, just in time for the French Admiralty to digest its implications before the outbreak of hostilities with Great Britain. It did not help them or their unfortunate transient allies. Cape St Vincent, Camperdown, the Nile, Copenhagen, and 21 October 1805 all lay ahead. And the guns that would sink French ships, including above all the fearsome, heavy and deadly 'carronade', were cast at Carron, Stirlingshire, using coal perhaps hewn from Clerk's mines.

JOHN CLERK, *Essai Méthodique et Historique sur la Tactique Navale*...translated by Daniel Lescallier (Paris, 1791)
AB. 5.76.7

4.12 The general and the guardsman

SIR RALPH ABERCROMBY was one of the great Scottish heroes of the Napoleonic wars. An important army reformer, he was loved by his officers and men. John Kay's portrait, one of hundreds done of his contemporaries in a distinctive style combining perception with naivety, shows Abercromby before the Pyramids, constructions Kay was evidently none too sure about and which, ironically, Abercromby himself never saw, not having reached Cairo. Abercromby died of wounds received in action at Alexandria in 1801 and has a fine monument in St Paul's cathedral. His death was noble: given a blanket, he asked whose it was; on being told it was 'only a common soldier's' he was horrified, and demanded that his ADC return it to the man immediately. The journal of a private soldier in the 3rd (Scots) Foot Guards at Alexandria sheds fascinating light on Abercromby's Egyptian campaign. Other ranks' diaries, though generally less well expressed and lacking the broader view, are more interesting than those of officers, being much rarer. Newman writes clearly, and with notable descriptive power, about wounds, death and hardship: the British seaborne assault at Aboukir Bay met stiff resistance, and Newman's 'landing craft' was sunk. He swam to a nearby boat, only to be beaten off on his colonel's order. Rather than seeking 'compensation' or pleading 'combat stress', Newman philosophically reasons that this (though the action seemed harsh at the time) was for the greater good of all,

as his (and others') coming aboard might have swamped the flatboat. No wonder General Abercromby was proud to command such resolute men.

JOHN KAY, *A Series of Original Portraits and Caricature Etchings*, 2 vols (Edinburgh, 1837) NC.240.a.1

Acc. 12054, journal of William Newman, 1799-1809

Page 18

not Swim — as it is generally Said. a Person when Drownding will Catch hold of any thing within their Reach ——
    I Very Soon Saw a boat loaded with troops Comeing from the fleet and Makeing for Shore — I Emediately Swam in an Oblique Direction So as it Could not Possibly Make land without Passing near to Me — I had now Some Hopes that by the Assistance of the Almighty I Should be Saved from the Jaws of a Devouring Sea — but what was My Disappointment — it had no Sooner Come upto me, then I Saw Colonel Dalrymple on board, who was My Commanding Officer — and I heard him Order one of the Sailors to beat

Page 19

Me under Water with one of the Oars if I attempted to Come on board — I Naturolley Considered his Order as a Very Severe one — but the fact was the boat was heavey Loaded. and as this was a time for Every one to look for himself he Surposed by taken Me on board it might be the Means of her Swamping and all hands Parishing — So that it was better to lose one Man then hazzard the lives of a boat load —— I was now Past all hopes, but willing to Struggle against Death as long as I was able — I took another Survay around Me — and at a Distance Saw a boat laying upon her Oars — I Emediately Made for her

4.13 'Bring forrit the tartan!'

THE HIGHLAND BRIGADE played a leading part in the British army's effort in the hard and often chaotic Crimea campaign. The 93rd (Sutherland) Highlanders were called the 'thin red streak tipped with a line of steel' as they faced the massed attack of Russian cavalry at Balaklava. William Howard Russell's original description became distorted into the 'thin red line', which then came to be applied generically to British infantry on any nineteenth-century battlefield. The Library's manuscript collections hold important Crimean material, not least the retrospective 'Notes and Recollections' of William Simpson, who covered the war as an artist for the illustrated periodical press of the day (Acc. 11877). Simpson's volume of lithographs is the major artistic product of the war. This view of the Highland Brigade camp shows Major-General Sir Colin Campbell within a bastion, the snowy Crimean landscape stretching away into the

distance. Campbell, a Glaswegian, was a great Victorian hero who joined the army young and poor, changing his name from Macliver to Campbell as the latter was felt to be 'a better name to fight under'. His remarkable career, which took him from the Peninsula to the Indian Mutiny via China, gained him a field marshal's baton and a peerage as Baron Clyde of

Clydesdale. The Victoria Cross was instituted to award bravery in the Crimea; the first army VCs were won by a sergeant and an officer of the Scots (Fusilier) Guards, the latter a member of the Crawford family, whose papers are in the Library.

WILLIAM SIMPSON, *The Seat of War in the East* (London, 1855)

EL.4.87.4

4.14
Preparing for the trenches

THE NAME OF Douglas Haig will forever be associated, however unfairly, with the bloody stalemate of the trench warfare of the Western Front in the First World War. Haig had prepared more thoroughly for high command than almost anyone else of his generation. This notebook dates from his time at Sandhurst in 1884. Recent wars then keenly studied were the American Civil War and the more recent and even more relevant Franco-Prussian War. The young Edinburgh-born officer-cadet's theoretical study of trench- and siege-warfare would acquire a new and very real meaning for the general 30 years later. The Haig Papers,

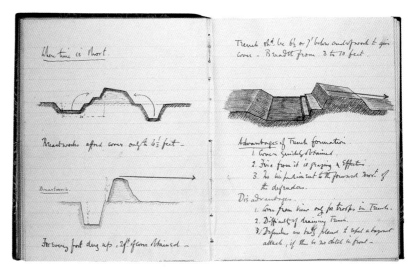

long held in the Library, were bought from the second Earl Haig in 1982. The archive constitutes the most important single source in Great

Britain for the conduct of the First World War and is heavily used by historians.

Acc. 3155/28

4.15 The Old Contemptibles

LIEUTENANT-GENERAL Sir Douglas Haig enjoyed marked royal favour and obtained one of the army's most prestigious posts when he was appointed GOC Aldershot Command. Highly desirable in peacetime, this also carried the wartime command of a major part of what would be a British Expeditionary Force in Europe. An album of photographs (the Haig Papers contain a wealth of photographic material) shows royal reviews and manoeuvres at Aldershot in the years immediately preceding the outbreak of hostilities: images of the old order that was about to change forever. Though small by European standards, the pre-1914 British army was well-trained, highly efficient, and at the very apex of its splendour in terms of the full-dress uniforms worn on such occasions as those recorded here. The new military world is symbolised by the appearance of aircraft of the Royal Flying Corps above the plumed hats of the mounted staff officers on parade. Many of the troops shown in the album would constitute I Army Corps, which Haig took to France in August 1914. These were the men whom Kaiser Wilhelm derided as a 'contemptible little army'. Proudly they turned an insult into an epithet of honour, and called themselves the Old Contemptibles.

Acc. 3155/43

4.16 'Maga' does its bit

BY THE TWENTIETH century *Blackwood's Magazine* (or *'Maga'*) had become, as it were, the house-journal of the British Empire. The strong critical bent of its early years had long since given way to a diet of tales of adventure and military life. Countless officers must have whiled away time in the trenches and dug-outs of Flanders, or in the wardrooms of the Grand Fleet, reading the latest monthly issue of *Blackwood's* in its severe, unchanging cover bearing the portrait of George Buchanan within a thistle-ornamented border. This copy allegedly saved one reader's life from a shard of high-explosive shell. In gratitude he sent it from Arras to the Edinburgh publishers, where it was treasured as a token of the special contribution of *'Maga'* to the war effort. However it seems that, rather than actually stopping the force of the shrapnel when in a man's pocket, the periodical had suffered its 'wound' less dramatically in some dark corner of a dug-out as its owner was on stand-to in the line. Nevertheless, the injury was sufficiently serious to be the longed-for 'Blighty one', a coveted passport out of action and back home to Britain and civvy-street. Recalled to the colours, *Blackwood's* was to survive another war, and was to limp on into lonely and protracted old age before expiring, last of a breed, in 1980.

MS. 30923

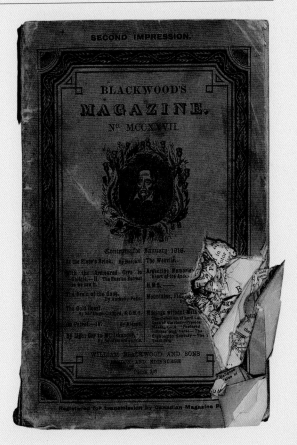

4.17 **Sturdy in Britain's defence**

HIRAM STURDY WAS a miner from the pit-village of Newarthill, near Motherwell, Lanarkshire. He had served in the First World War, and in the Second was in the local Home Guard. Sturdy's illustrated diaries of the war period are as fascinating as the rest of his remarkable record (in many slim volumes) of life in a close-knit community. This stylish watercolour, showing the influence of international art movements with which Sturdy must have been familiar, has about it the look of a work by the English futurist painter Christopher Nevinson. Sturdy was for a time a house-painter and may have read about, and looked at illustrations of, painting of a different sort. The composition encapsulates the entire war effort; both the younger fighting men in the field abroad, and the night-time anti-aircraft or security duty undertaken by older men such as Sturdy at home. Sturdy's albums would make a book by themselves; they are exceptional historical and social sources.

Dep. 279/43, on deposit from the Sturdy family

4.18 Blue bonnets over the border

THE ACQUISITION OF the papers of Peter White has furnished the Library with an important Second World War archive to join many collections relating to the conflict. These range from the papers of Major-General Douglas Wimberley, who commanded 51st (Highland) Division at Alamein, and those of his successor, Major-General James Scott Elliot, through the records of individual units such as the yeomanry regiment the Lothians and Border Horse, to the diaries of John Telfer Dunbar, who had the misfortune to endure long years of Japanese captivity. White was a schoolboy at the outbreak of war, and became an art student at the Royal Academy schools. Overcoming earlier pacifist tendencies, he joined the army and was commissioned into the

Royal Artillery, but transferred to the infantry and was posted to the 4th Battalion, King's Own Scottish Borderers. This formed part of a so-called Mountain Division, which (as was frequently the paradoxical way of things) was sent to Holland. His illustrated diary chronicling his platoon's advance through Holland and into Germany in the hard fighting of the harsh winter of 1944-45 is already established as a classic of modern military literature. It had remained unpublished and unknown after Peter White's death in 1985, but its eventual appearance as *With the Jocks* in 2001 gave the world a remarkable book by an exceptionally perceptive writer. White's schoolboy diary, copiously illustrated, remains unpublished.

Acc. 12886

Scotland and the New World 5

5.1 'Upon a peak in Darien'

THE 'COMPANY of Scotland trading to Africa and the Indies' was established in 1695. The glowing hopes for it were evident in the crest granted, a sun in splendour rising from the waves. The *Rising Sun*, of Greenock, would later be one of the ships that sailed to Darien and disaster. In its time the Company of Scotland was never known as the 'Darien' Company; but so central did the ill-fated attempt to establish the colony on the central American isthmus become in the tragic history of the company and its people, that all its varied activities appeared to be summed up in that one word. The first expedition went out to Darien from Scotland in 1698; two others followed. Scotland had had a 'colony' before; in 1621 Nova Scotia was its own New

World. But now there was a real wish to have a proper colony, and therefore a market overseas. Mismanagement, over-optimism, climate, disease, Spanish hostility and English intransigence and refusal to help – all brought financial ruin and death. The company's books and papers are in the Library. This contemporary map of 1699 shows the colony of New Caledonia. It comes from the Yester Papers of the first Marquess of Tweeddale, Lord High Commissioner when the company was established. Although Scottish flags can be made out, the scale is too small to see the detail of the settlement of New Edinburgh, with Fort St Andrew. These can be appreciated in other, later maps in the Library.
EMAM. s. 48

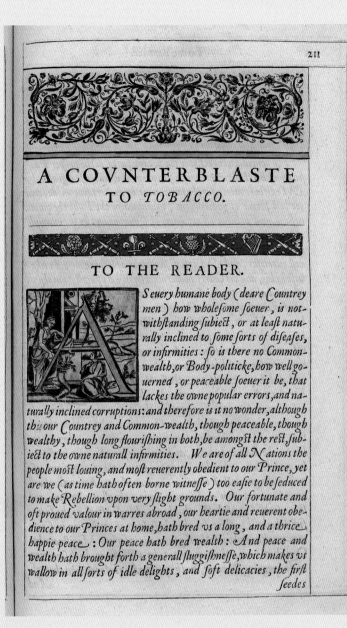

A COVNTERBLASTE
TO *TOBACCO.*

TO THE READER.

As euery humane body (deare Countrey men) how wholesome soeuer, is not-withstanding subiect, or at least natu-rally inclined to some sorts of diseases, or infirmities : so is there no Common-wealth, or Body-politicke, how well go-uerned, or peaceable soeuer it be, that lackes the owne popular errors, and na-turally inclined corruptions: and therefore is it no wonder, although this our Countrey and Common-wealth, though peaceable, though wealthy, though long flourishing in both, be amongst the rest, sub-iect to the owne naturall infirmities. We are of all Nations the people most louing, and most reuerently obedient to our Prince, yet are we (as time hath often borne witnesse) too easie to be seduced to make Rebellion vpon very slight grounds. Our fortunate and oft proued valour in warres abroad, our heartie and reuerent obe-dience to our Princes at home, hath bred vs a long, and a thrice happie peace : Our peace hath bred wealth : And peace and wealth hath brought forth a generall sluggishnesse, which makes vs wallow in all sorts of idle delights, and soft delicacies, the first seedes

5.2 To smoke or not to smoke?

THE SCHOLARLY King James VI and I published *A Counterblaste to Tobacco* just after acceding to the throne of England and moving south, to a court where tobacco is said to have been popularised by Sir Walter Raleigh; he was supposed to have brought it, with potatoes, from America – though James never wrote a book on tatties. The *Counterblaste* was reissued in the magnificent edition of the king's collected works of 1616. This copy, with the royal arms on the binding, and with ornaments and initial letters picked out in colour, was once thought to have been James's own. The title-page is a remarkable, if confused and fantastic, masterpiece of Jacobean taste (or tastelessness) in decoration. Tobacco-taking was a 'vile custome', not introduced from a 'godly, necessary or honourable ground', but rather out of 'base corruption and barbaritie' and an 'inconsiderate

and childish affectation of Noueltie'. Why should Englishmen or Scots 'imitate the barbarous and beastly maners of the wilde, godlesse, and slauish *Indians*'? Risking royal disapproval, a Scottish doctor, William Barclay, published in Edinburgh in 1614 a small book, *Nepenthes, or The Vertues of Tabacco*, which took a diametrically opposite view from his sovereign. Barclay praised the medicinal properties of the plant, and advocated smoking 'with emptie stomack, not as the English abusers do, which make a smoke-box of their skull…then to carie the braine of him that can not walke, can not ryde except the *Tabacco* Pype be in his mouth'.

The Workes of the Most High and Mighty Prince, James (London, 1616)

Ry. III. a. 11

ONE COULD HARDLY invent the life of Peter Williamson. Kidnapped aged 10 in Aberdeen by a merchant; transported to the American plantations; sold on to another Scot in Pennsylvania; given a farm, only to be captured by Indians in league with the French; served in the British colonial forces, and wounded; prosecuted for libel by the Aberdeen merchants for having written the book shown here; fined, banished from Aberdeen and his book publicly burned; his case for reparation successfully taken to the Court of Session; and so on. *French and Indian Cruelty* is his best-known book, and one frequently reprinted over many years, with a portrait frontispiece of the hero in exotic Indian frontier costume. A Paisley edition in 1816 has a wildly inaccurate frontispiece, showing the author being burned at the stake by sixteenth-century Spaniards dressed for the Inquisition! Williamson also produced a useful Edinburgh street directory, which is of sociological importance in analysing the class-structure of the city. A coffee room he opened in Parliament House in the 1770s, Indian Peter's, served the readers of the Advocates' Library of the day. John Kay (cf. 4.12) produced a double portrait of Williamson with James Bruce of Kinnaird, the African traveller (cf. 6.3), entitled 'Travells Eldest Son in Conversation with a Cherokee Chief'. In the caption Williamson says that he may never have eaten a lion, but that his *Edinburgh Directory* was of more use to mankind than Bruce's five volumes.

French and Indian Cruelty; Exemplified in the Life and various Vicissitudes of Fortune of Peter Williamson (Edinburgh, 1762)
ABS.1.88.208

PETER · WILLIAMSON
In the Drefs of a Delaware Indian.
1 Tomohawk.   5 Powder horn.
2 Scalping Knife.   6 Indian Canoe.
3 Shot Bag.   7 Bush Feighting.
4 Purse & Belt of Wampum 8 War Dance.

Acc 8389

St Petersburgh March 1/12 1777

Dear Sir Charles

I sincerly & heartily Congratu-late You, on your return from your Suc-cessfull Campaigne in Canada, and the honours & Title His Majesty has been pleas'd to distinguish you with, for your Vigorous & Important Services. — I would fain hope that such another suc-cessfull Campaigne in America as this last has been, (notwithstanding the lateness of its opening) will put an end to this unhappy & disagreeable War. I cannot help thinking but the dasterdly behaviour of the Rebels hitherto, shews them to be very unworthy of that Liberty & Inde-pendance which they urge as the specious Pretence of their Rebellion. — Should this Rebellion be crush'd (which I hope in God it will) without their standing one deci-sive Battle, they'll make but a rediculous figure in history. — Your Expedition in building Vessels on the Lake, as Mr Baxter Informs me, almost surpasses belief

5.4 Damned rebels – and useless at that

'FORCEFUL' MIGHT DESCRIBE this letter of 1777 from one Scottish admiral (albeit in the Russian service) to another who had just saved Canada from the clutches of the American revolutionaries – forceful, if not foreseeing. Samuel Greig, from Inverkeithing, Fife, discontented with slow promotion in the Royal Navy, took the opportunity to transfer to the Russian fleet. There he rose quickly, receiving from Catherine the Great many chivalric orders and the rank of grand admiral. He is regarded as the father of the Russian navy, in which many of his fellow officers were Scotsmen. His correspondent, Captain Sir Charles Douglas, had pushed through the ice of the St Lawrence to relieve Quebec in 1776 and received a baronetcy for his efforts. Greig expresses the hope that another successful campaign in America may 'put an end to this unhappy & disagreeable war. I cannot help thinking but the dastardly behaviour of the Rebels hitherto, shews them to be very unworthy of that Liberty & Independence which they urge as specious Pretence of their Rebellion. Should this Rebellion be crush'd (which I hope in God it will) without their standing one decisive battle, they'll make but a ridiculous figure in history.'
Acc. 8389

5.5 'A name remarkable in Europe and magic in America'

THE WEST LOTHIAN-BORN Robert Liston (1742–1836) was one of the most remarkable British diplomats of his age. The spines of the volumes of his papers in the Library give evidence of his myriad postings: he served almost everywhere a British minister plenipotentiary could serve, including two terms in Constantinople. In 1796 he was sent to Washington, where he remained until 1802. His wife Henrietta was an indefatigable diarist and letter-writer. Open-minded, tolerant and good-natured, Mrs Liston was generally impressed by all she saw and met: here both President Washington and the First Lady are praised, he as 'the most perfect idea, in person, dress & manners, of a true Republican', she as a woman of kindness. Many British diplomatic wives might have been much less pleasant and more condescending; Harriet Liston somewhat more charitably wrote of Martha Washington whose 'figure, though short & fat, is not without dignity, her face retains the marks of delicate beauty & her voice is melody itself'. The next year Mrs Liston (MS. 5590, f. 40) would see Washington on the celebration of his birthday, which was an occasion as nearly akin to a royal one as the US could support. The president wore uniform and the Order of Cincinnatus, the institution of which, smacking of 'hereditary honor', had been controversial and was confined to wear by a very few surviving recipients on this day alone. Harriet Liston's journals contrast with the acerbic, superior tone

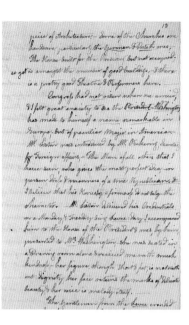

of that written by Francis Jeffrey in 1813 (Acc. 11099), where much mockery is made of American country-bumpkin manners.

MS. 5696

5.6 Unflattering images of North America

CAPTAIN BASIL HALL, RN, belonged to a family noted for curiosity in science and the arts. The records of the European travels of his father, Sir James Hall, president of the Royal Society of Edinburgh (cf. 8.17), and of his younger brother, James, a gentleman painter (cf. 7.8), are in the Library. Basil Hall travelled very widely, to rather more exotic locations than the others. North America was merely one of many parts of an expanding world he got to know, for he had explored Far Eastern and South American seas and coasts. The publication that resulted from his North American travels (1829) was controversial: Americans took marked exception to his views of their customs. As an accompaniment to his narrative, Hall published an album of etchings of people and places (most of them disagreeable, or disagreeably portrayed) after drawings made by himself with a *camera lucida*. Hall points out that the Mississauga Indian chief wears a silver medal of George III, given for 'service in old times'. The papoose at the right is described as a 'child strapped up in a box'. 'These little wretches', writes Hall archly, 'are sometimes hung upon the branches… or suspended on pegs in the wigwams, as may suit the convenience of the Squaws…This Indian plan of keeping young folks out of the way of mischief, might perhaps be adopted with advantage in countries east of the Atlantic.'

BASIL HALL, *Forty Etchings, from Sketches made with the Camera Lucida in North America in 1827 and 1828* (Edinburgh and London, 1829)

Nha. Misc. 101

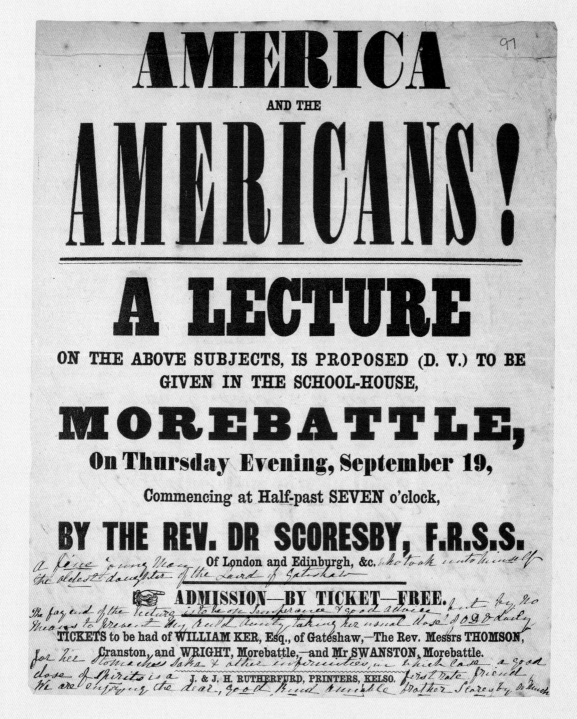

AMERICA
AND THE
AMERICANS!
A LECTURE
ON THE ABOVE SUBJECTS, IS PROPOSED (D. V.) TO BE GIVEN IN THE SCHOOL-HOUSE,
MOREBATTLE,
On Thursday Evening, September 19,
Commencing at Half-past SEVEN o'clock,
BY THE REV. DR SCORESBY, F.R.S.S.
Of London and Edinburgh, &c.

A fine young man who took into himself the oldest daughter of the Laird of Gateshaw

☞ ADMISSION—BY TICKET—FREE.

The fag-end of the lecture is to be on Temperance & good advice but by no means to prevent my Rudd Aunty taking her usual dose' DDD & Laily

TICKETS to be had of WILLIAM KER, Esq., of Gateshaw,—The Rev. Messrs THOMSON, Cranston, and WRIGHT, Morebattle,—and Mr SWANSTON, Morebattle.

for her stomaches sake & other infirmities, in which case a good dose of Spirits is a first rate friend

J. & J. H. RUTHERFURD, PRINTERS, KELSO.

We are enjoying the dear, good kind amiable Weather Scoresby so much

5.7 Lecture from America

MOREBATTLE IS A small and fairly remote border village on the edge of the Cheviots, some miles from Kelso, Roxburghshire. From the date on the poster (though no year is given), and from knowledge of the lecturer's biography, one can work out that the event took place in 1850. William Scoresby was a master-mariner and whaler, a Greenland and polar navigator of some distinction, and an expert in arctic geography, meteorology and magnetism. Having read chemistry and natural philosophy at Edinburgh he turned to theology and took a DD. The rather sarcastic comments added in manuscript appear to be a kind of gloss by one of Dr Scoresby's hearers or would-be hearers. The speaker was then aged 61, hardly a 'fine young man'. Whether or not the 'fag-end of the lecture' was really devoted to 'temperance and good advice', the village wit used the occasion as an excuse for some heavy-handed humour about an elderly aunt's fondness for the rum bottle.

L. C. Fol. 78 (97)

A CIVIC MUSEUM AND OUTLOOK TOWER FOR AN AMERICAN CITY. F.C. MEARS, ARCHITECT, EDINBURGH

5.8 One better than 'Greek' Thomson

'A SKYSCRAPER IN somewhat imperial American style' is how the architect and town-planner (Sir) Frank Mears described this design for a projected civic museum *cum* outlook tower for an unnamed US city. Mears was son-in-law to the visionary town-planner and sociologist Sir Patrick Geddes, whose papers in the Library are an important source on these subjects. The Geddes Papers include a letter from Mears of 1923 which incorporates a thumbnail sketch for this eclectic building. Attempting to deflect criticism, Mears suggests that Geddes will 'probably not quite like it', and argues that it is 'aimed at the American taste – heavy tower below…breaking out above into colonnaded temple

& turret.' (MS. 10573, f. 144). This large-scale pen and wash drawing is probably the worked-up design to which Mears refers in the letter. Mention of an outlook tower is interesting, for Geddes was the originator of the Outlook Tower or *camera obscura* on the Castlehill in Edinburgh, a high-minded tourist attraction with a difference, which is still in operation today. But unlike this, Mears's proposal drew inspiration from one of the seven wonders of the (ancient) world, the mausoleum at Halicarnassus, with elements of other buildings and details added for good measure; the 'campanile' at the right is believable early twentieth-century New York.
ACC. 11024

4

Government House
Ottawa

Mr. King to join him in the swimming pool, an offer which Mr. King
hastily
instantly refused. These two eminent men, neither of whom possesses
an elegant figure, wallowing in the White House swimming bath would
have been an excellent subject for an historical painting!

One result of the Treaty is that we shall probably have an
official visit from the President early next year. Lord Bessborough
had already been in negotiation on this point; but it was necessary
have some peg to hang it him on, such as the Reciprocity Treaty. Mr.
Roosevelt seems very keen to pay us a visit, and do something while in
America the President has even less before

I am greatly struck, Sir, by the intense royalist atmosphere
of Canada. There is no place in the world where Your Majesty is more
beloved, and that is true of the French just as much as of the English
population. The French, indeed, seem to have joined loyalty to Your
Person with their historic loyalty to their own ancien regime, and
M. Flandin told me that when he was here a year ago, for the Jacques
Cartier celebrations, he was amazed to see in Quebec vast placards, with
the legend Vive le Roi, and decorated with the fleur-de-lis! He natur-
French
ally rubbed his eyes and thought of a monarchist restoration in his
own country.

I anticipate a busy life here, but a most pleasant one.
Canada has some very intricate problems before her, but she is facing
them in the proper mood. The Ottawa people are most cordial, and I
yet because a victim
do not think I have been made a subject of the celebrated Ottawa gos-
from
sip, but I do not know with what private vices I may presently be
credited.

5

Government House,
Ottawa.

The British elections seem to have gone exactly as we had
very much as we
hoped effected. The Opposition will be reasonably strong, which is all to the
good, and there have been no serious casualties among the Government
followers.

May I venture to hope that Your Majesty's health is immune
dismal
from the discomforts of this awkward time of year?

I am, Sir,

Your Majesty's

Most humble, loyal, and devoted
subject,

5.9 A governor-general's letters to three kings

JOHN BUCHAN's long careers as both writer and believer in the British Empire appear to coalesce in the letters he wrote regularly as governor-general of Canada (November 1935-February 1940: he died in office) to his sovereign. When, created Lord Tweedsmuir of Elsfield, he went out to Ottawa, he was not to know that he would serve three monarchs. George V died in January 1936, Edward VIII abdicated, and was a succeeded by George VI. Buchan's private letters (this volume contains his own typed drafts with extensive manuscript corrections) contrive to be much more than reports of government.

They have the quality of literature and they are written, right from the start, with an appealing and unusual blend of deep respect tempered with affection, even familiarity. Some, such as the account of the Canadian prime minister, William Mackenzie King's visit to Washington in 1935, or of President Roosevelt's visit to Quebec the next year, are wry and very amusing. The three kings, none known for his literary taste or intellect, must have enjoyed reading these racy accounts of their representative's activities as antidote to much else in the day's red boxes.

Acc. 11738

Exploration, Adventure and Empire

6.1 From an antique land

To David Roberts, more than to any other individual, belongs the credit for making first the Holy Land, and thereafter Egypt, familiar to the Victorian public. Roberts was born in Edinburgh in 1796 and is the Scottish artist best represented in the Library's manuscript collections: his correspondence and papers have been acquired systematically since 1935, and the Library now has by far the greatest documentary holdings in the world relating to the painter and his circle. Roberts began as a theatrical scene-painter, and this background remained evident in his approach to the actual landscapes and real monuments he recorded in a life of exotic travel. He extended his interests from Scottish scenery and antiquities to northern Europe, thence to Spain and North Africa, and then Egypt, Sinai, Palestine and the Levant. Oddly enough, Italy, which might have been expected to have cast its spell on him as on other artists, came relatively late to his mind and eye. Roberts published

three volumes of drawings, superbly lithographed by the Belgian Louis Haghe, of the Holy Land and Syria between 1842 and 1849; his *Egypt and Nubia* appeared, also in three volumes, between 1846 and 1849. They made him and his publisher, Francis Graham Moon, a fortune and they have ensured Roberts's lasting fame as the interpreter of the Near East *par excellence*. Cheap reproductions of his plates may be bought today throughout the countries he visited – modern Jordan, Israel, Lebanon, Syria and Egypt. His journeys can be followed in the surviving two-volume manuscript journals of his Near Eastern travels (Acc. 7723 /1-2). This plate, showing the Pyramids and Sphinx at Giza, with a scorching desert wind or *simoom* blowing up, is, despite its topographical inaccuracy, one of the most dramatic and 'theatrical' of all Roberts's views.

David Roberts, *Egypt and Nubia*, vol. III (London, 1849)

K. 117.b

Loe here's mine Effigie, and Turkish suite;
My Staffe, my Shassc, as I did Asia foote:
Plac'd in old Ilium; Priams Scepter thralles:
The Grecian Campe design'd; lost Dardan falles
Gird'd with small Simois: Idaes tops, a Gate;
Two fatall Tombes, an Eagle, sackt Troyes State.

6.2 Cut-lugged Willie on the road

ALTHOUGH SCOTSMEN had travelled before him, and were to be keen adventurers long after his time, William Lithgow, from Lanark, was the first to make a real impact as a travel writer. 'Adventurer' is a loaded designation and usually implies a raffish element; Lithgow was known as 'cut-lugged' Willie because sheep-shears had been used on his ears by the brothers of a girl he had made pregnant. He spent 19 years walking through Europe, Asia and North Africa, totalling (he said) 36,000 miles in 'three deare bought Voyages' encompassing 'innumerable toyles, pleasures, and inevitable sorrowes'. He always walked, shunning all conveyances, expect when crossing water – when he condescended to take boat or ship. Lithgow also shunned modesty, in his prologue commending his work to the 'wise', the 'profound historian' and the 'understanding Gentleman'. Rather oddly and anti-climactically, his wonderful book ends with an account of a 'pedestriall progresse' back home in Scotland, where he roundly condemned the destruction of ancient buildings in the name of religion as 'knocking all down to desolation; leaving nought to be seene of admirable Edifices, but like to the Ruines of *Troy, Tyrus,* and *Thebes,* lumpes of Wals, and heapes of stones'. We see him making the point in his frontispiece, pictured before the ruins of Troy, with a charming verse epitome of the iconography and emblematic meaning of the portrait. This is probably the first image of a British traveller to be depicted with classical ruins, an association that became a commonplace and a status-symbol in the age of the Grand Tour.

WILLIAM LITHGOW, *The Totall Discourse, of the Rare Adventures, and Painefull Peregrinations of Long Nineteene Yeares Travayles, from Scotland...* (London, 1632)

H.32.a.10

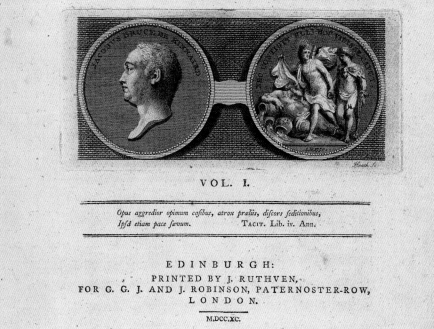

TRAVELS

TO DISCOVER THE

SOURCE OF THE NILE,

In the Years 1768, 1769, 1770, 1771, 1772, and 1773.

IN FIVE VOLUMES.

BY JAMES BRUCE OF KINNAIRD, ESQ. F.R.S.

VOL. I.

Opus aggredior opimum cafibus, atrox præliis, difcors feditionibus, Ipfâ etiam pace fævum.   TACIT. Lib. iv. Ann.

EDINBURGH:
PRINTED BY J. RUTHVEN,
FOR G. G. J. AND J. ROBINSON, PATERNOSTER-ROW,
LONDON.
M.DCC.XC.

6.3 The pale Abyssinian

ALTHOUGH JOHN OGILBY, who never actually set foot in the Dark Continent, is regarded as the father of Scottish 'Afric-ology' with his *Africa* of 1670 (its introduction has a delightful headpiece engraved by Wenceslaus Hollar), it is James Bruce of Kinnaird who stands at the top of the long and distinguished list of Scottish explorers. Bruce was a larger-than-life character, physically and in every other way. Truly a kenspeckle figure, he is shown in conversation pieces and group portraits such as Zoffany's *Tribuna of the Uffizi* towering over his contemporaries. He was the first modern traveller to attempt to solve the enduring question of the source of the Nile. His expedition took him down the Red Sea and inland though Ethiopia. The resulting account of his travels and discoveries of 1768-73 was one of the largest travel books of his,

or later, times. Edinburgh publication was rapidly followed by a German edition issued in Leipzig the same year. In a remarkable example of faithful translation, Bruce's maps, re-engraved, have every detail of geographical feature and place-name rendered into German: only the original dedication to the king is omitted for the German market. The medal which decorates the title-page shows the head of Bruce himself on the obverse, while on the reverse is an allegorical design of Apollo and the young Heracles (perhaps allusive of Bruce's personal physical power and stature) unveiling the covered head of the Nile river-god.

JAMES BRUCE, *Travels to Discover the Source of the Nile*, 5 vols (Edinburgh, 1790)

K.180.a

6.4 Through Africa in the kilt

A Waltz with a Hippopotamus.

ROUALEYN GORDON-CUMMING lived to kill. An Old Etonian army officer who served briefly in three continents, he stalked, shot and hooked anything that moved – whether at home in Scotland (he came of the landed family of Altyre and Gordonstoun, Elgin, whose papers are in the Library), in North America, or above all in South Africa, where, between 1843 and 1848, he conducted a wholesale campaign of slaughter of big game. He once recorded that it took him an hour, and 57 rounds, to finish off a bull elephant. The best-selling book shown here has several illustrations of his exploits with very big and very wild animals, which make it all seem deceptively easy. Above the whimsical caption 'A Waltz with a Hippopotamus', the woodcut shows his attack, with a very small knife, upon the huge beast in the water, the bearded and long-haired Scotsman holding onto the animal's tail. In

South Africa, Gordon-Cumming habitually wore the kilt and no stockings on campaign on the veldt, as his ox-wagon train followed. He was a lion-hunter *par excellence*, and was 'lionized' by the British public. This book later appeared in a condensed version, stressing particularly the lion-hunting element: this followed his successful display of trophies at the Great Exhibition, itinerant showings of his lion-skins, and a successful lecture-programme. Having survived all manner of encounters with dangerous animals, he died, aged only 46, at Fort Augustus, Invernessshire, where he had established a museum. A premonition had caused him to order his coffin just beforehand.

ROUALEYN GORDON-CUMMING, *Five Years of a Hunter's Life in the Far Interior of South Africa... and Anecdotes of the Chase of the Lion, Elephant, Hippopotamus, Giraffe, Rhinoceros, etc.*, 2 vols (London, 1850)
K. 181.f

6.5 Ottoman observations

HENRY ASTON BARKER was dispatched to Constantinople to paint a view of the fabled city for his father's Panorama House in London. This expedition necessitated a winter voyage through the Mediterranean in wartime. At the end of 1799 his ship put in to Palermo, where Barker encountered Nelson, Sir William and Lady Hamilton, and the Neapolitan royal family in exile. Barker's journal records some wry comments on the relationship between Nelson and Emma Hamilton, and nar-

rates how the admiral amused himself after dinner (when Emma cut his meat, which he could not easily do for himself, having only one hand) by teaching the Neapolitan princesses what they took to be 'English blessings' but which were in fact naval imprecations. Barker went on to the Ottoman capital and recorded not only some striking views of its inhabitants, but also some of the goings-on in Lord Elgin's embassy. Scots were no strangers to Constantinople. Sir Robert Ainslie had been British ambassador there 25 years previously, and later sponsored fine illustrated accounts, by Luigi Mayer, of the Ottoman dominions, while Sir Robert Liston later represented His Britannic Majesty at the Sublime Porte.

Barker Papers, MS. 9650

Elephants in quicksand crossing arm of ye Ganges in pursuit of a tiger. TWT

Tiger seizing elephant at Sattorypore on the Ganges. TWT 1809

6.6 Passion and pig-sticking

THE HUGE ARCHIVE of the distinguished Roxburghshire family, the Elliots of Minto, includes the papers of two governors-general of India. The first Earl of Minto was governor-general between 1807 and 1813. His descendant, the fourth earl, followed Lord Curzon as viceroy from 1905 to 1910; he had already served as governor-general of Canada. The Minto Papers contain material relating to every aspect of Indian imperial administration, and illustrate British life in India over these two periods a century apart. From the time of the first earl's governor-generalship comes this letter from his military secretary, Captain Thomas William Taylor, later Major-General Sir Thomas Taylor, addressed to the governor-general's daughter, Lady Anna Maria Elliot. Clearly the young officer was sweet on her. But in a series of beautifully illustrated letters he may have stressed too much the sporting life of pig-sticking, tiger-shooting and the other pursuits of the British soldier or civilian involved in the taking and running of an emerging empire. There were other things she might have preferred to hear, beyond Captain Taylor's prowess in the hunting field, or see, beyond his skill as an amateur water-colourist. Much later the lady married Sir Rufane Donkin, who was slightly older than Taylor, slightly better-connected, slightly cleverer, and a lieutenant-general to the bargain. Promoted general, Donkin subsequently hanged himself. Maybe Taylor would have been the safer bet in the end.

Minto Papers, MS. 11102, f. 120

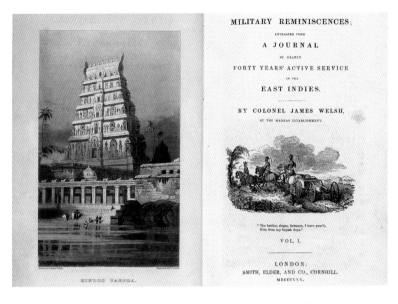

siege and storming of Ahmadnagar in August 1803 prior to the battle of Assaye highlights one of the minor tragedies of the story of the Scottish soldier in India. Two officers of the 78th Highlanders had quarrelled over a trifling matter of honour and etiquette. One was an older and less fortunate officer, English by birth; the other, a younger, promising but more headstrong man. The latter 'borrowed' the former's company piper without asking formal consent. Insults and a duel ensued, in which Captain Browne, the senior, was killed. Captain Duncan Grant, let down by his second, was placed under close arrest. Seeking to restore his good name, he broke from his escort and rushed first up a scaling-ladder at the enemy fort, only to be shot dead. Two decent officers were therefore lost, when their service in battle might have been valuable.

JAMES WELSH, *Military Reminiscences; Extracted from a Journal of Nearly Forty Years' Active Service in the East Indies*, 2 vols (London, 1830)

E. 143.b

6.7 Forty years service – and eighteen more to follow

THE MILITARY CAREER of James Welsh was characteristic, if not perhaps typical, of Scottish soldiers of the East India Company's army. His *Reminiscences* were published (by Smith, Elder and Co., a firm directed by London Scots and which later merged with the house of John Murray) during a period of furlough at home, breaking a remarkably long life of service in the East. Commissioned into the Madras Infantry in 1790, he retired to Bath as a lieutenant-general in 1847. The illustrations in his book are his own. He served under Arthur Wellesley, the future Duke of Wellington, at Seringapatam, and took part in the Mahratta War. Welsh's account of the

6.8 Like border reivers

FOUNDER OF A FIRM of Indian agents which dealt with the transport of passengers and their astonishing quantities of baggage, Captain Robert Melville Grindlay went on to establish the bank bearing his Scottish family name. Grindlay, who later also concerned himself with the matter of steam communication with India, and thus with the very sinews of empire, was author of *Hints for Travellers to India* (1847). This offered practical guidance on routes to be chosen (depending on the level of security and comfort expected, or the degree of risk acceptable) or on to what to pack for service or leisure-travel in the East. The question of communication, especially in the region of the future Suez Canal, pre-occupied many Scots. But, prior to all this, Grindlay had published an opulent part-work entitled *Scenery, Costumes and Architecture chiefly on the Western Side of India* (1826-30). This proved so expensive to produce that the original publisher, Rudolph Ackermann, gave up on it; after some negotiation with Blackwood of Edinburgh, Grindlay managed to persuade Smith, Elder & Co. to take it on to completion. This plate shows the Rajah of Cutch and his vassals. Grindlay draws the parallel between such feudal bands and those of Border chiefs and clans 'so vividly depicted by the classic pen of Sir Walter Scott'. Martial bearing, habits, feuding, loyalty and heroism all 'might afford a fertile theme for such a minstrel'.

E. 144. a. 9

6.9 (Gaol) birds of Australia

ON TWO KNOWN OCCASIONS Sir Walter
Scott helped or encouraged Scottish wrong-
doers to make new lives in Australia.
George Harper and Ebenezer Knox had got
on the wrong side of the law and ended up
in Botany Bay. In circumstances not entirely
clear, Scott was able to assist them in starting life afresh. Both prospered in
agriculture. In Knox's case, Scott had inter-
vened on his behalf with Governor Lachlan
MacQuarie, known for his liberal policies
and his willingness to help convicts to new
lives, and a free pardon was procured. Knox
wrote a letter to Scott expressing gratitude
in terms that are unintentionally and amus-
ingly patronising. Harper's gratitude for the
new circumstances he enjoyed via Scott's
recommendation to Sir Thomas Brisbane
took more material form. He wrote offering
Scott some characteristic Australian
wildlife: two kangaroos, a brace of black
swan or a pair of emus. Wanting, in all honesty, none of these, Scott plumped for the
'emuses' – which he assumed were the size
of parrots. Scott's horror when Harper and
the emus arrived at Leith docks, the birds
alive and standing 'six feet high on [their]
stocking soles', led to some highly amusing
correspondence with his publisher, Robert
Cadell. Scott even feared least they devour
his precious collection of armour at Abbotsford. A notion to send the creatures to the
Royal Menagerie at the Tower of London,
thus shunting the problem onto the king,
came to nothing. They ended their days in
the Duke of Buccleuch's Dalkeith Park.

Cadell Collection, MS. 744, f. 180–180v

To

J. Keir Hardie M.P.

Leader of the British Parliamentary Labor Party

Dear Comrade.

On behalf of Organised Labor of this Western State of the Commonwealth, we extend to you a hearty welcome to this Continent as a representative of our comrades in Great Brittain.

We can assure you that throughout Australia you may rely upon receiving from the workers that enthusiastic welcome that befits one who has done so much for the movement and who occupies such a proud position in our organisation.

6.10 **More Aussie wildlife, and a wild socialist**

JAMES KEIR HARDIE remains one of the heroes of working-class Scotland, and indeed of the United Kingdom. A miner who turned to socialist journalism and trade-union organisation, he founded the Scottish Labour Party and subsequently became, in 1892, the first Independent Labour MP at Westminster – though not, ironically, for a Scottish constituency. He was widely known as 'the man with the cloth cap'. Hardie travelled extensively through the British dominions and India in support of trade-union and socialist ideals. He advocated the liberation of blacks in South Africa, and supported Indian independence. On his visit to India he was shadowed by the authorities, and police reports (preserved in the Library's Minto Papers) were compiled about his movements and contacts. On a tour of western Australia he was presented with this illuminated address, strangely reminiscent of the kind of document that might be offered by organisations of a different stripe to visiting dignitaries of a somewhat different social status; 'comrade' is not a term one expects to see in such things. The animals and birds of Australia, supporting the shield of arms, recall the offer of these creatures to Walter Scott (cf. 6.9), a man of utterly divergent political views, 80 or so years before.

Keir Hardie and Emrys Hughes Papers, Dep. 176, Box2/7

CAPTAIN AYLMER HALDANE of the Gordon Highlanders served in the Waziristan and Tirah expeditions, on the north-west frontier of India, in 1894-95 and 1897-98. In his diary (later typed when he prepared his memoirs as a knighted general) he recorded his regiment's participation in the celebrated action at the heights of Dargai, where the Gordons succeeded in capturing a strongly-held position which the Dorsets, Derbyshires and Gurkhas had failed to take. Here Piper George Findlater won the VC, playing his battalion forward to the regimental quick march 'Cock o' the North', though lying wounded in both legs. Haldane himself made the initial recommendation for this award to yet another Scot, General Sir William Lockhart, commanding the expeditionary force. Haldane served subsequently in the Boer War, and was captured in the episode of the armoured train at Chieveley, Natal – an incident made famous by the involvement of an impetuous war-correspondent named Winston Churchill. Haldane and Churchill were taken to Pretoria and interned. They planned to escape from a latrine but only Churchill got out. Haldane long resented this, seeing it as some sort of betrayal on the part of Churchill, who subsequently described how he had leapt from a water-closet to international fame. (In Haldane's journal, Churchill is confusingly abbreviated to 'W.C.'!) Sir Aylmer later moderated his views, however, recognising that the man who had stymied his escape-attempt had mutated into the saviour not just of his own young skin but, in 1940, of Europe's.

Aylmer Haldane Papers, MS. 20247, f. 128

6.12 From the St Lawrence to the Nile

BEFORE HE BECAME viceroy of India in 1905 (cf. 6.6), the fourth Earl of Minto had been governor-general of Canada (1898-1904). Before that again – as Viscount Melgund – he had served the Marquess of Lansdowne, then governor-general of Canada, as his military secretary (1883-85). Melgund had served in the Scots Guards and had soldiered in various capacities in Afghanistan, South Africa and Egypt; as an observer he had also witnessed war in Spain, Turkey-in-Europe and during the Paris Commune. His time in Canada coincided with the crisis in the Sudan, when a major expedition had to be mounted in an attempt to relieve General Gordon at Khartoum. Melgund hit on a scheme to employ French Canadian boatmen (*voyageurs*) to man craft on the Nile expedition. Many of these men must have been of questionable loyalty to the crown, and the scheme was a bold one: representatives of one of Britain's oldest imperial problems were to be recruited and transported halfway round the world to help solve a very new one. Melgund's papers contain draft terms of employment and conditions for these *Métis*, and telegrams in not very sophisticated cipher where, for example, 'take charge of small boats in rapid water' was rendered as 'tapestry chastise of smouldering boats in ratiocination weekly'. But within months Melgund was absorbed by the suppression of Louis Riel's north-western rebellion, a domestic Canadian crisis emphasizing the enduring problem of French-Canadian disaffection.

Minto Papers, MS. 12549, ff. 2-3

6.13 A viceroy's sweet tooth

THE VICEREGAL PAPERS of the second of the Minto governors-general of India contain vast quantities of material covering every aspect of the life and administration of the sub-continent. For example, there are intelligence reports of tribal activity on the frontier, military dispatches detailing wounds suffered by individual British soldiers, and wonderfully exotic volumes preserving letters on very grand writing-paper from Indian princes offering greetings to the viceroy, often in the most high-flown and unconsciously amusing terms. The Minto Indian papers also include substantial quantities of household accounts for the viceregal establishments in Calcutta and Simla, from which can be deduced the tastes of the very popular and well-regarded viceroy and his charming vicereine. They clearly liked the traditional British breakfast of Arbroath smokies, kippers, porridge, Oxford marmalade, and copious quantities of Victory ham, caviar and Cheddar cheese. Other, more exotic, delicacies came from local suppliers such as Haran Chunder Coondoo & Gosto Behary Biswas; while Framjee of Simla supplied crackers, chocolate and mixed sweets on an invoice endorsed 'Band picnic'. The viceroy himself was rather partial to chocolates supplied by Federico Peliti of Calcutta, Simla and Naini-Tal. How did this 'Tallie' from Turin (as an Italian ice-cream seller might have been known back in Hawick) end up there?

Minto Papers, MS 12695 (ii), f. 514

6.14 'Auld Reekie, still and on!'

THIS LETTER OF Robert Louis Stevenson was written from Samoa to the fifth Earl of Rosebery, at that time foreign secretary and soon to be prime minister – and, much later again, one of the National Library's most important benefactors. The letter is misdated by one month: it is actually from December 1893. As befits a recipient who was both politician and bookman, it addresses both subjects. Rosebery had sent a copy of Stevenson's *Catriona* to its author, in his South Sea exile, for inscription; the two had been corresponding about Samoan politics. Here Stevenson (once called to the Scottish Bar) opens with a Scottish legal term, *as effeirs*, that is 'in due form'. Rosebery had evidently said something about the Lothian landscape that had touched RLS's heart and mind. He explains that there was much that would prevent his return to places he loved, yet where he had formerly been 'vigorously unhappy'. Many of the friends of his youth were 'lapped in lead'. But, however painful the prospect of return, he would nevertheless like to be buried there, 'among the hills, say, on the head of Allermuir – with a table tombstone like a Cameronian'. Stevenson the exile would never return, in life or in death, which claimed him two days short of a year later. 'Here's where he lies where he longed to be', he wrote in a famous epitaph of longing for Scotland – one that was carved, not on a Scottish tomb, but on his grave on Mount Vaea.

Rosebery Papers, MS. 10091, f. 168

THE PIPER AND THE PENGUIN.

6.15 Polar piobaireachd

THE LIBRARY HAS LARGE and important collections which render it a major centre for polar – especially Antarctic – and alpine studies. The Scottish National Antarctic Expedition set out in 1902 in the whaler *Hekla*, now renamed the *Scotia*. The protagonists believed 'it may be that, in endeavouring to serve humanity by adding another link to the golden chain of science, we have also shown that the nationality of Scotland is a power that must be reckoned with'. The published record of the expedition includes the delightful photograph of 'The Piper and the Penguin', showing Piper Kerr playing to a bird which remained unmoved by 'rousing marches, lively reels or melancholy laments': 'we had no Orpheus to warble sweetly on a lute… there was no excitement, no sign of appreciation or disapproval, only sleepy indifference'. Few humans, surely, react to the pipes with such detachment.

In the course of British Antarctic exploration a tradition was established of producing shipboard newspapers: Scott's *South Polar Times* and the later, more regular, *Aurora Australis* remain the best known. Produced in limited quantity, some surviving sets of the latter are bound in boards of a kind of plywood that once contained provisions for Shackleton's Nimrod expedition of 1907-09; the 'bindings' of the Library's copies read 'Honey' and 'Fruit'. The printer's device was two penguins. The periodical contained a mixture of original work, one of the stories being a rather droll one by a Scottish doctor to the expedition, Alasdair Mackay, entitled 'Interview with an Emperor', in which poachers encounter a penguin 'gamekeeper' of markedly Scottish speech and manner.

The Voyage of the Scotia (Edinburgh, 1906)

Wordie. 235

Taste, Travel and Antiquity

7.1 The draughtsman who looked up

GEORGE RICHARDSON began as a humble draughtsman in the office of the Adam brothers. He accompanied James Adam to Rome in the early 1760s, and recorded his experiences – the most formative of his life – in two significant letters preserved in the Library (MS. 3812, ff. 1-5). He continued to work for the Adams for some years after his return from what had effectively been a Grand Tour, though one of an unusual sort, in that he had undertaken it in the service of a man of higher station, sharing vicariously an experience that would otherwise have been denied him. He rose to become an architect in his own right, but more especially a successful and well-regarded author of influential works on aspects of architectural design and decoration. Of these, his *Book of Ceilings* was the best known. As a decorative designer,

Richardson worked in what we think of as the elegant, sophisticated and eclectic 'Adam style'. To him may be attributed a book of neoclassical designs for ceilings and wall decoration also in the collection (MS. 2876). He worked for some of Robert Adam's major patrons, and his own subscription lists are impressive in bringing together many of the leading figures in architectural practice and patronage of the day. The design shown was executed for the dining room of Sir Lawrence Dundas's town house in St Andrew Square, Edinburgh, 1774. Coloured copies of Richardson's book are rare and desirable.

GEORGE RICHARDSON, *A Book of Ceilings, Composed in the Style of the Antique Grotesque* (London, 1776)
FB. el. 132

7.2 'To learn *bon ton* and see the world'

In this line from 'The Twa Dogs', Burns captured the essence of the cultural and social phenomenon we know as The Grand Tour. This period of European travel and adventure in an eighteenth-century gentleman's education was ostensibly intended for the acquisition of a little learning, some taste and manners, and a passing familiarity with the art and architecture of the classical world. However, it was all too often, in reality, an extended 'gap-year' experience of rather less high-minded pleasures. Despite this, the importance of the Grand Tour for Scotland and the Scots can hardly be over-emphasised. The Library holds an original manuscript version of what became the first great travel handbook for Grand Tourists, Richard Lassels's *Voyage of Italy*, originally written for a Scottish nobleman (Adv. MS. 15.2.5). The Library's

printed and manuscript collections for the study of the Grand Tour are important and extensive and have been much increased in recent years, for example by the acquisition of the volume of letters of Roger Robertson shown here. Robertson was the best sort of traveller, one genuinely interested in art and antiquity, books and manners. He wrote long letters to his father, often in French or Italian, to show that he had learned something, assuring him that he was neither over-spending (the commonest parental complaint) nor keeping bad company (the perennial parental worry), even in Venice, which was the notorious 'brothel of Europe' at the time. His descriptions of Pompeii and Herculaneum in the early 1750s are particularly interesting.

Acc. 12244

7.3 Dreams (or nightmares) of ancient grandeur

A MORE POTENT influence upon eighteenth-century taste can hardly be imagined than the vision of ancient Rome conceived by Giovanni Battista Piranesi, and marketed through his etchings of the monuments and artefacts of the Eternal City. His *Vedute di Roma* series is justly famous, although many travellers were disappointed by what they actually found in Rome after being inspired by the prints, where scale is magnified and perspective distorted for picturesque effect. Even more influential with antiquaries and architects was Piranesi's *Antichità Romane*, a vehicle for the artist's personal crusade to magnify, in the most grandiloquent terms, the achievement of the Romans at a time when scholars looked increasingly to Greece as the fountainhead of western art and architecture. Robert Adam hugely admired this work, as he did

much else of Piranesi's *oeuvre*. The two were friends when Adam was in Italy in the 1750s. The upwardly-mobile Scot was ever anxious to push himself forward, and to appear as both a leading antiquary learned about the past, and as a man who could use antiquity for his own professional ends, as an architect and designer working in the present and for the future. Piranesi helped him in various ways involving propaganda, more or less subtle. The Scottish painter and aesthetic theorist Allan Ramsay was also of this circle, and he and Robert Adam both feature in this plate, where Piranesi sets their imagined tombs (bearing laudatory 'epitaphs') along the Via Appia in a fantastic jumble of mind-blowing unreality.

GIOVANNI BATTISTA PIRANESI, *Le Antichità Romane*, 4 vols (Rome, 1756), second frontispiece to vol. 2. N.68

7.4 Madam, I'm Adam

EVEN MORE EXTRAORDINARY tribute was paid to Robert
Adam alone, but much more blatantly, in Piranesi's superb
Campo Marzio. Through a forceful combination of personality,
genuine ability and the power of money – all of which helped
direct the engraver's burin – Adam was able to extract remarkable tributes, in the form of allusions in some of Piranesi's most
astonishing plates. The deal was that Adam took quantities of
copies of the work in question for re-sale in Britain. It was all
part of his determined campaign of self-promotion; biblio-
graphic tributes such as this were a very useful 'marketing' tool,
promoting Adam as both learned antiquary and thrusting
young architect. Piranesi's extraordinary folio on the ruins of
the Campus Martius district of ancient Rome contains no less
than five magnificent plates which trumpet the name of Robert
Adam as if he were some imperial Roman hero commemorated in time-worn inscriptions. These range from 'altars' and
sarcophagi bearing or associated with the Scotsman's name,
through vast imaginative reconstructions of what this part of
Rome might have looked like, to 'aerial' views of the actual
remains, bearing decorative borders of 'antique' fragments
among or upon which the name of ADAM is dramatically
superimposed. Nothing else quite like this brazen propaganda
exercise exists in the entire history of British art or taste.

GIOVANNI BATTISTA PIRANESI, *Il Campo Marzio dell' Antica Roma*
(Rome, 1762). N. 68

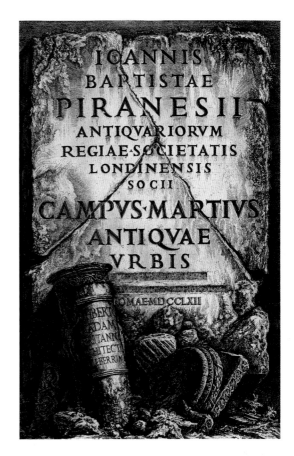

7.5 Herculean labours at Herculaneum

ALLAN RAMSAY, the painter, was the first to spread news of the discoveries at Herculaneum by translating and publishing, in the *Philosophical Transactions* of the Royal Society of London in 1740, some letters on the subject by his friend, the Neapolitan painter Camillo Paderni. The bibliography of the subsequent 'official' publications on the antiquities unearthed at Herculaneum since its discovery in the 1730s is rather complex, with divergent titles and general confusion among volumes, but this need not compromise our enjoyment of the books as fine examples of the printer's art. They record the artefacts, wall-paintings, etc., which had been removed from the site to the Bourbon royal museum at Portici outside Naples. They were handsomely produced at the royal press of the Kingdom of the Two Sicilies, under the very imperfect direction of Ottavio Antonio Bayardi, whose plodding scholarship was widely derided as 'burying the ancient world of Herculaneum beneath a much denser veil than that spread over it by the lava'. Despite this, the Faculty of Advocates was anxious to complete its set of volumes, which King Ferdinand of Naples had graciously begun to present (retrospectively) to the Advocates' Library in 1766 – testimony to its international standing as a scholarly collection strong in contemporary antiquarian material of this kind. A suitably grateful address was returned to his Neapolitan majesty, and this was followed by entreaties in the highest political and diplomatic circles to keep the books coming to Edinburgh, regardless of war or peace. Scottish Grand Tourists were drawn to the excavations and the Portici museum as moths to a candle.

Le Pitture Antiche d'Ercolano (Naples, 1757)
E.129.b.11

7.6 Advocating the antique

CHARLES-LOUIS CLÉRISSEAU was a French architect and draughtsman who taught a succession of British architects, notably Robert Adam, to see classical antiquity in a new way and to draw the ruins of the past in a most evocative and compelling fashion. Adam, who met him in Florence and who took him to Rome as what might now be called a 'personal trainer', owed Clérisseau a great deal in perfecting his manner of rendering ruins and *capriccii*. It was Clérisseau who drew the picturesque views for Adam's great folio *Ruins of the Palace of the Emperor Diocletian at Spalatro in Dalmatia* (1764), though Adam meanly denied him any credit for his work and left the reader to imagine that all he saw was the product of Adam's own picturesque genius. By way of riposte, Clérisseau insinuated his name into the text of 'Roman' inscriptions included in some of these plates; Adam never noticed that he had been duped in this way. Clérisseau's own projected work on the Roman antiquities of southern France, which so many British Grand Tourists saw as their first taste of classical buildings in a former Roman province, never progressed beyond this first volume, on the splendid monuments of Nîmes. The Faculty of Advocates acquired this copy before 1787, and the Faculty's large-scale *ex libris* inscription insouciantly succeeds in stealing some limelight from the so-called 'Temple of Diana' on this page.

C. L. CLÉRISSEAU, *Antiquités de la France: Première Partie, Monumens de Nismes* (Paris, 1778)

A. 83.a

THE COLLECTING OF classical coins and gems was an important aspect of the culture of the renaissance and the centuries that followed. For learned men of the period, these small works of art and antiquity were valued for the commentary on literature, mythology and history they afforded. The Faculty of Advocates had a collection of ancient coins worth more than passing notice, and also a collection of 'sulphurs' - that is, casts of gems and intaglios. The Faculty also possessed the first Egyptian mummy to have come to Scotland: this arrived in 1748, and survived in an increasingly disreputable state in the National Library's vaults until 1958, when it was given to a Glasgow anatomist for dissection. A superb Louis XV cabinet by Charles Cressent was acquired in 1777 for the Faculty's coins at what was even then a bargain price: this was inexplicably sold for a ridiculously small sum in 1873. The emblematic frontispiece by David Allan to the catalogue of James Tassie's collection of gem casts, dated Edinburgh 1788, symbolises the ethos of virtuoso collecting: Athene sits on a Greek chair, before a medal cabinet of magnificent, if unusual, neoclassical design, her Gorgon shield on the floor next to the famous bust of 'Homer' that was itself an emblem of British collecting in the seventeenth and eighteenth centuries.

R. E. Raspe, *A Descriptive Catalogue of a General Collection of Ancient and Modern Engraved Gems...* (London 1791)

E. 52. b. 5

7.8 **The dying speech of a pencil**

OF ALL THE LIBRARY's Grand Tour diaries, perhaps the most delightful is that by James Hall. It is late in date (1821-22), incomplete (the Spanish volumes are lost), and written in fading pencil. But where else in the literature of the Grand Tour is the tourist's own writing-implement itself commemorated? Hall, son of Sir James (cf. 8.17) and younger brother of Basil (cf. 5.6), was an advocate who soon abandoned practice at the Scottish Bar for the life of a gentleman painter and dilettante. It was he who, in 1850, presented the manuscript of *Waverley* to the Advocates' Library (cf. 10.5). His journal of travel in France, Italy and Germany is strikingly written, frequently in the present tense, and is illustrated with hundreds of minute sketches done on the spot or in motion; Hall labels them with code-letters to indicate his method, 'D.O.S.' or 'D.I.M.', etc. On one occasion he even drew the pencil that had just given up the ghost. Below a D.O.S. sketch of its inert form he wrote: 'This is the last effort and dying speech of a pencil, which has lasted till daylight can be seen below the lead. His brother stump died yesterday… he now dies in writing his own epitaph!'

MS. 27626, f. 75v

E. A. P. del.

7.9 Victorian archaeologists 'at home'

THIS DELIGHTFUL VIGNETTE of archaeologists relaxing in a rock-tomb near the Fountain of Apollo at Cyrene, with photographic equipment, and with as many creature comforts as were necessary to make it a temporary home-from-home, ornaments a page of a work describing a British government-sponsored archaeological exploration in north Africa. The Royal Engineers officer involved, Kilmarnock-born (Sir) Robert Murdoch Smith, was already experienced in this field, having commanded the sapper detachment on the expedition to Asia Minor which discovered the site of the legendary mausoleum of Halicarnassus and transferred to the British Museum the sculpture adorning that structure. Smith had been instrumental in the identification of the site. He turned his attention

to Cyrenaica, and the material discovered there was likewise sent to the Museum. Scottish involvement with the antiquities of north Africa can be traced to the work of James Bruce of Kinnaird in Algeria a century before (cf. 6.2). After a distinguished career directing the imperial telegraph service in Persia, Smith became involved in museum administration as director of the Edinburgh Museum of Science and Art (the Royal Scottish Museum). One of his daughters married a scholarly advocate, William Kirk Dickson, who became the last Keeper of the Advocates' Library and, in 1925, the first Librarian of the National Library of Scotland.

R. MURDOCH SMITH and E. A. PORCHER, *History of the Recent Discoveries at Cyrene...* (London, 1864)

E. 150. a. 17

Thought, Music, Art and Architecture

8.1 The British architect

THE TRIUMPH IN architecture of Scottish designers of the eighteenth century was one of the great national achievements. After the Union, several Scottish architects emerged as leaders of taste and fashion in an England they had taken by storm. The first was Colen Campbell, who had previously practised as an advocate in Edinburgh. He became associated in about 1713 with a London publishing venture which was already under way. *Vitruvius Britannicus*, in its three volumes of 1715, 1717 and 1725, became the most celebrated British architectural publication of the age. It was enlivened with a selection of designs by Campbell himself, paying tribute to the inspiration of the great Andrea Palladio; these followed plates illustrating works by the masters of English baroque, such as Wren, Vanbrugh and Hawksmoor. Campbell's introduction praises the 'Antique Simplicity' of Palladio and, by extension, the work of the great English neo-Palladian progenitor, Inigo Jones, which he contrasts with the 'capricious… affected and licentious … wildly extravagant' forms of the Italian baroque. Campbell came to enjoy significant patronage and designed many influential buildings, especially great country houses and smaller villas, and none more so than Wanstead in Essex, shown here in its executed design. He was instrumental in carrying through the 'Palladian revolution' in British architecture. William Adam was inspired by Campbell's example to attempt to collect specimens of Scottish architectural design, culminating in his own vigorous works, in what appeared in 1811, long after his death, as *Vitruvius Scoticus*. *Vitruvius Britannicus, or the British Architect…*, vol. I (London, 1715) A. 86. c

(Page 7.)
List of the Members of the select Society.

1754

pr. Mr John Jardin Minister of the Gospel in Edinburgh.
pr. Dr Francis Hume.
pr. Mr Adam Smith Professor at Glasgow.
+ Mr Anderson. +
pr. Mr Alexander Wedderburn.
pr. Mr Simon Fraser Advocate.
pr. Mr Alan Ramsay Painter
pr. Mr James Burnett Advocate.
pr. Mr John Campbell Advocate.
pr. Mr Alexander Carlile Minister at Inveresk.
pr. Mr William Johnston Advocate.
pr. Mr James Stephenson Rogers Advocate.
pr. Mr David Hume.
pr. Mr John Swinton Advocate.
pr. Dr Alexander Stephenson.
pr. Mr Patrick Murray Advocate.
pr. Mr Patrick Hume of Billie.
pr. Mr Walter Stewart Advocate.
pr. Mr John Hume Minister at Athelstanford.
pr. Mr Robert Alexander.
pr. Mr James Russel Surgeon.
pr. Mr George Cockburn Advocate.
pr. Dr David Clarke.
Mr George Brown Advocate.
pr. Mr William Robertson Minister at Gladsmuir.
Mr John Fletcher.
pr. Mr Alexander Agnew.
pr. Dr John Hope.
Sir David Dalrymple Advocate.
Mr Gilbert Elliot Advocate.
Sir Harry Erskine.
Mr Hugh Blair Minister.
Mr Andrew Stewart Writer.
June 12. Mr Charles Fish Palmer.
pr. Mr George Morison.
pr. Mr George Dempster.
June 19. Mr Andrew Pringle
pr. Mr Alexander Monro
pr. Mr David Ross

Pat.

8.2 'The éclat of our Scotch literati'

IT WAS A SOURCE of some puzzlement even to the leaders of what we now call the 'Scottish Enlightenment' that a small, poor, and relatively backward country on the north-western edge of Europe should, quite suddenly, find itself catapulted into the very forefront of western thought, and to a position of cultural and scientific leadership in every field, from chemistry, medicine, geology and engineering, to philosophy, historiography, architecture and *belles lettres*. From the mid-eighteenth century to the death of Walter Scott in 1832, Scotland was an intellectual centre of world significance. One of the conduits of intellectual life was the network of social and literary clubs in the Scottish cities, which brought together academics, clergymen, lawyers, merchants, industrialists, and other men of enterprise and drive. Of these institutions, perhaps the most distinguished was the Select Society, founded in Edinburgh in 1754 by the painter Allan Ramsay, himself a characteristic 'Enlightenment' figure. This met in the rooms of the Advocates' Library. Its minute-book preserves a record of its debates, and of those who attended and presided. It also lists candidates for, and admissions to, the coveted membership of what David Hume described to Ramsay as a 'national concern', and James Adam a body that redounded to 'the *éclat* of our Scotch *literati*'.

Adv. MS. 23.1.1

8.3 A book to pass away the time

THE WORLD OF THE Scottish Enlightenment was club-
bable, and the *literati* generally got on well with each
other in conviviality and mutual respect. Most notable of
all these friendships was that between David Hume and
Adam Smith; its record is preserved in the greatest of all
archives relating to the Scottish Enlightenment. This is
the correspondence of David Hume, which belongs to the
Royal Society of Edinburgh, itself a child of the Enlightenment, and which is on long-term deposit in the
Library. Hume had once hoped to succeed Smith in his
first chair (of logic) at Glasgow, but had been appointed
Keeper of the Advocates' Library in 1752, a post he
described as 'a genteel office, though of small revenue'.
Having used the Library's books in the writing of his celebrated *History of England*, Hume found both fame and
fortune in Britain before being tempted to Paris in 1763
as secretary to the British ambassador. He was there, the
toast of the *salons* and lionised as 'le bon David', when
Smith, much less happily placed in France, wrote this letter. He had quit his chair in moral philosophy at Glasgow
in 1764, and was employed as tutor to the young Duke of

Buccleuch in France and Switzerland. Conditions in
which to cultivate the mind and senses were not readily
forthcoming. The Duke knew no Frenchmen and Smith
was limited in the intercourse he could promote. 'The life
which I led at Glasgow', Smith confides to Hume despon-
dently in this letter from Toulouse, 'was a pleasurable,
dissipated life in comparison of that which I lead here at
Present. I have begun to write a book in order to pass
away the time. You may believe I have very little to do.'
Great oaks… The book was to evolve into *An Enquiry
into the Nature and Causes of the Wealth of Nations*, published in 1776 to universal acclaim and enduring fame.
The Hume collection includes highly important docu-
ments such as his letter of congratulation to Smith on the
publication of *The Wealth of Nations*, and Hume's brief
manuscript memoir, 'My Own Life', composed as he was
dying. This, with its final passages touchingly written in
the past tense as if death had already claimed him, constitutes one of the finest and certainly the shortest
autobiographies in the English language.

Hume Papers, MS. 23157, no. 32

8.4 The true scene for a man of letters

A SENSE OF THE affection between Hume and Smith, and of Hume's *bonhomie* and wit, is encapsulated in this letter which, together with other correspondence preserved in the Library, relates to the publication of *The Wealth of Nations*. Hume wished to know what had happened to this book, already printed but not yet published: 'If you wait till the Fate of America be decided, you may wait long.' Smith was expected to move from Kirkcaldy to Edinburgh. 'Your Chamber in my House is always unoccupied: I am always at home: I expect you to land there.' If Smith delays his arrival, Hume may be dead: his sudden dramatic weight loss may cause him to 'disappear altogether'. The crisis in America is not so important as is commonly imagined; but a reading of Smith's book may cause Hume to alter his opinion. Then comes the concluding sally of wit from the man who was so much at ease in Paris, and who regarded Edinburgh as the true scene for a man of letters: 'Shoud London [due to commercial damage resulting from loss of trade with America] fall as much in its size, as I have done, it will be the better. It is nothing but a Hulk of bad and unclean Humours.'

Hume Papers, MS. 23152, no. 55

8.5 The approbation of Scotch historians

AMONG THE PAPERS of William Robertson – divine, university administrator and historian of Scotland, of Charles V and of America – is to be found this very flattering letter from Edward Gibbon. The historian of the decline and fall of the Roman Empire reports to Robertson of the current success in France, in the translation by Suard and Jansen, of Robertson's *History of America* – a book that had become 'a favourite subject of conversation'. Robertson had been fortunate in his timing. He was engaged in his study when the American Revolution broke out, and it is interesting to note (in the part of the manuscript of this book which is preserved in the Library as MS. 3965) which historical events of the past were being dealt with on particular dates when contemporary history was being made. Gibbon's letter of 1777 opens with a statement of admiration for Robertson and Hume, 'two names which friendship united and which posterity will never separate'. 'When I ventured to assume the character of historian, the first, the most natural, but at the same time the most ambitious wish' had been for their approbation. Gibbon ends by sending greetings to two further luminaries of the Scottish Enlightenment, Adam Ferguson and Adam Smith. His comment on the distinction of Scottish historiography echoes Hume's

observation, made in 1770 to his London printer-publisher William Strahan, himself a Scot, that 'this is the historical Age and this the historical Nation'.

Robertson-Macdonald Papers, MS. 3943, ff. 28-29v

8.6 Carving a musical reputation

ROBERT CARVER, born about 1484, is perhaps the first outstanding name in Scottish music. His choir-book, or antiphonary, is called variously after the composer himself or his Augustinian abbey of Scone in Perthshire (Carver was a canon of Scone as well as being a musician in the Chapel Royal at Stirling). It preserves a selection of masses and motets by contemporary English and continental composers, and it also contains works by Carver himself. As such, it is one of the very few extant music manuscripts to survive from pre-Reformation Scotland – a place of some cheerfulness, as the decorations in the choir-book indicate. No other source exists for Carver's own work, which he was contributing to this collection as late as 1546; indeed, of the whole manuscript's 24 compositions, 18 are otherwise unknown. Carver and his antiphonary provide the inspiration for the 1988 motet by the contemporary composer Ronald Stevenson, 'In Memoriam Robert Carver' (Acc. 11471). The Carver choir-book entered the Advocates' Library before 1819, having been in the collections of William Tytler of Woodhouselee, a lawyer of poetical and musical interests, and his son, the judge and historian, Alexander Fraser Tytler, Lord Woodhouselee. The elder Tytler was celebrated for his prescription for a happy old age: 'short but cheerful meals, music, and a good conscience.'

Adv. MS. 5.1.15

8.7 Music-making in the shadow of Arthur's Seat

1724 WAS A SIGNIFICANT year for Scottish literature. Allan Ramsay published *The Ever-Green*, his anthology of early Scottish poetry, mostly drawn from the Bannatyne Manuscript (cf. 10.12), and he also brought out the first volume of his collection of popular verse, *The Tea-Table Miscellany*. This contained a mixture of traditional songs and ballads, uncritically edited and altered by himself, and verse of his own composition. The title of his compilation reflected the Augustan taste of his day and echoes the spirit of *The Spectator*. Ramsay's decision to promote the Scottish language, and his great success in so doing, was of critical importance for the poets who followed, notably Robert Fergusson and Robert Burns. However, the songs of *The Tea-Table Miscellany* were published without music. Traditional tunes to accompany them were rapidly provided in attractive arrangements by William Thomson in his *Orpheus Caledonius*. Ramsay's riposte was to commission Alexander Stuart, an Edinburgh fiddler, to set his *Tea-Table* songs to appealing airs. Richard Cooper, an English engraver recently settled in Edinburgh and who would soon become involved with Ramsay's literary and artistic circle, supplied a delightful image of a fashionable musical couple before a window giving a view of the Edinburgh landscape. This plate shows Ramsay's appeal to the middle and upper classes as well as to the common people, from whose tradition many of the songs actually came.

ALEXANDER STUART, *Musick for Allan Ramsay's Collection of Scots Songs* (Edinburgh, c. 1725)

Inglis.38

8.8 Music across the social divide

THE APPEAL OF MUSIC for very different elements in Scottish society is illustrated by these images of widely contrasting kinds of musical performance. John Harden was an Ulster landowner and amateur artist, who in 1803 had married the daughter of Robert Allan, Edinburgh banker and proprietor of the *Caledonian Mercury*. Jessy Allan's letters to her sister in India were illustrated with drawings by Harden of the family's life in their elegant New Town house in Queen Street. Musical performance was a major element in these drawings; it was by far the most important domestic activity of the Harden circle. Domestic entertainment frequently involved chamber concerts and more informal music-making. Harden's sketches often show contented couples at the harpsichord or with the violin, in comfortable surroundings, as others read or play cards in the soft circles of candle-light. This example is typical. In a very different social context in the following century, Hiram Sturdy, the miner from Newarthill, Lanarkshire (cf. 4.17), records this musical fellow-miner playing his fiddle prior to the start of his shift, 'in his pit claes, coalie lamp and big tackitty bits before going to the Blackie'. Sturdy's journal text informs us that Rab was keen, and good enough to pass the examination as Associate of the London College of Violinists. Though sharing a common interest, it yet remains unlikely that he and his sort would ever have made music with the Hardens or their ilk.

Harden Drawings, MS. 8867, II.1.A

Sturdy Papers, Dep. 279/ 36

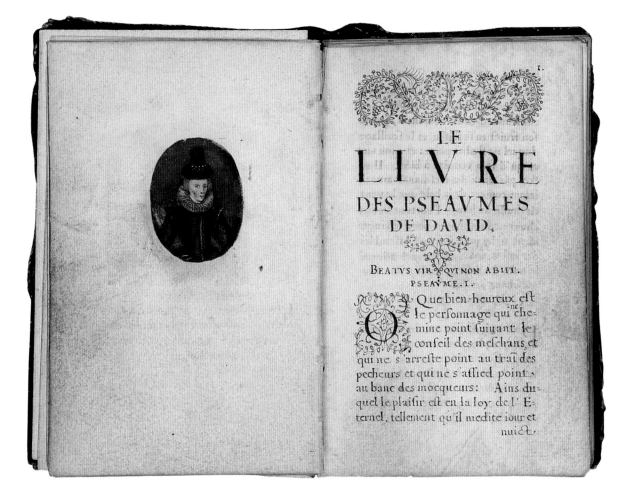

8.9 A miniature vision of faith and art

THE EXQUISITE WORK of the early seventeenth-century calligrapher Esther Inglis has long been admired, and the Library holds a distinguished group of her manuscripts, including examples of the various kinds of miniature illuminated books in which she specialised. She often worked speculatively, offering her books to patrons in the hope that they would be tempted by what they saw. Esther Inglis was the daughter of a French Huguenot refugee. Born in London, she came to Edinburgh at an early age. Her father was master of the French school, and taught handwriting; her mother was skilled in penmanship. But Esther outclassed them by far, becoming a calligrapher of

international reputation. Her mastery of a wide range of hands and styles (including mirror writing) was remarkable, as was her ability to work to the minutest scale. While some of the Library's Esther Inglis manuscripts display much greater variety of script and are much more beautifully illuminated, that shown here has the interest and attraction of including a self-portrait, perhaps the earliest of or by a woman artist in Scotland. The book, here shown magnified, is dedicated to King James VI and I: it has an embroidered binding of silver thread on mulberry velvet, featuring a phoenix design, probably her own work.

MS. 8874, 'Les Pseaumes de David', 1615

8.10 Old Masters for Scotland

THE MANUSCRIPT COLLECTIONS of the Library are rich in material relating to the vigorous trade in Old Master paintings in which – particularly in the early nineteenth century – Scottish artists, dealers, connoisseurs and collectors were active participants, and sometimes leaders of taste and commerce. The correspondence and papers of William Buchanan, James Irvine, David Stewart and Andrew Wilson are major sources of information. So, on occasion, are letters from the painter David Wilkie, who, after David Roberts, is probably the artist best represented in the manuscript collections. Italy was the great hunting-ground, though not all the pictures were by Italian masters. In this case the quarry was Van Dyck. Wilkie was in Genoa in 1827

and there he came across wonderful pictures which their impoverished owners seemed disposed to sell if the offer were good. The Van Dycks in Genoese collections were splendid works and would clearly be much appreciated in Britain, where the artist was both influential and venerated. In the bottom left corner of this letter to Andrew Wilson, Wilkie has drawn a thumbnail sketch of *The Lomellini Family*, adding the succinct comment: 'Genoa will furnish capital material for you.' He was right. In 1830 Wilson succeeded in buying this great group-portrait of about 1626, showing the then doge's family, for the Royal Institution in Edinburgh, ancestor of the National Gallery of Scotland.

MS. 3812, f. 8

ALBUM·VON·DRESDEN·UND· ·SÄCHSISCHE·SCHWEIZ·

8.11 The Glasgow Style – and not by Mackintosh

THE ART OF Charles Rennie Mackintosh, the outstanding *fin de siècle* Glasgow designer, is now so well-known as to be something of a cliché. All manner of tourist tat makes a 'Mockintosh' of his style. The Library holds many of the continental publications in which his designs were first made known to an admiring Europe: the influential periodical *Dekorative Kunst*, which first drew attention to the Glasgow school; Alexander Koch's portfolio devoted to 'Toshie' in the *Meister der Innen Kunst* series, in which the designs for a 'House for a Lover of Art' were published; and *Deutsche Kunst und Dekoration,* with the Hill House, Helensburgh, designs. But he was not alone in inventing and promoting a distinctive Scottish *art nouveau* style. His younger

contemporary Jessie Marion King was, and remains, highly regarded in many of the same areas, though the larger and more dramatic field of architecture was outside King's rather more limited range. Book illustration, however, was a refined and gentle realm in which she attained particular distinction, appealing to those attracted by her inspiration in the world of fairy-tale and legend. Notable is her series of cover designs for books published by Globus Verlag of Berlin. The exterior and interior of this book do not quite marry: outside, fey girls with plaits and pigtails; inside, indifferent photographs of Dresden townscape and Saxon countryside.

Album von Dresden und Sächsische Schweiz (Berlin [1899])

FB. m. 124

8.12 The complete artist

JAMES PITTENDRIGH MACGILLIVRAY possessed not
only one of the most difficult names in the Scottish art-
world for 'foreigners' to pronounce or spell, but also a
prodigious talent in many fields. A distinguished career
brought official recognition as Sculptor-in-Ordinary
for Scotland. In this role he produced much fine and
distinctive work, and many drawings and sketches for
his commissions are preserved among his voluminous
papers in the Library. Macgillivray was also a poet.
Bog Myrtle and Peet Reek (1922), privately printed and
looking as if this had been done in 1722, is his major
contribution to the verse tradition of Scotland, whose
cause he sought to advance though his interest in
nationalism. In all these areas Macgillivray is representative of a movement in the Scotland of the 1920s aimed
at re-discovering the country's identity through literary,

artistic and political self-expression, and perhaps
above all through the imaginative use of the powerful
Scots language. People talked of a 'Scottish Renaissance'. Interestingly, the Library's copy of *Bog Myrtle*
(X.191.a) was presented and inscribed by the author in
February 1925 to 'The National Library of Scotland' –
nine months before that was a legal entity, a move
indicative of what the new institution, then in process
of establishment, was already being taken to symbolise
in terms of revived national consciousness. In this
caricature, by an unknown artist, Macgillivray appears
as a 'Renaissance man' of a kind, with the symbols of
his art and calling about him, himself on the pedestal
as a dancing faun, and with an umbrella to shield him
from the Scottish weather.

Macgillivray Papers, Dep. 349/217

Duff House & Town of Banff

8.13 Duff House, but no duff architect

IN THE 1730S William Adam was commissioned to design and build a house on the outskirts of Banff for William Duff, later Lord Braco and later still Earl of Fife. This might have been a northern palace to rival Hopetoun in West Lothian, but acrimonious disputes culminated in 1743 in a lawsuit between patron and architect. Adam had a tendency to let costs run up, and to blind his clients with architectural 'learning'. The quarrel resulted in the building remaining a disproportioned 'tower', without the quadrants and pavilions that Adam proposed and which are illustrated in *Vitruvius Scoticus*: these wings would have had the effect of lessening the overwhelming verticality of the baroque centrepiece. Thirty years later, John Woolfe and James Gandon, who jointly published a two-volume continuation of Campbell's *Vitruvius Britannicus* in 1767 and 1771, proposed a scheme for providing the

lonely centre block with wings, but once again these remained paper dreams. This watercolour by Charles Cordiner, an Episcopalian clergyman in Banff, is one of those inserted in an extra-illustrated copy of his book on regional antiquities and scenery: it records the house and its improbable setting, a huge baroque pile rising in parkland on the edge of a small Banffshire fishing and harbour community, but with a fine classical Gibbsian church for company. Cordiner wrote of the house in the expectation that the wings would indeed be added. Duff shows Adam at his most exuberantly showy and, though it is by no means his finest achievement, it is certainly distinctive and vigorous.

CHARLES CORDINER, *Antiquities & Scenery of the North of Scotland, in a Series of Letters to Thomas Pennant* (London, 1780)

F.7.d.1

8.14 The world's pattern book

A Book of Architecture by James Gibbs was arguably the
most influential British architectural publication of all
time. The author, an Aberdonian Catholic who had
trained in Rome under Carlo Fontana, was immersed in
the Italian baroque; he was therefore outside the Palladian pale of Campbell's circle. But through his patron, the
Jacobite Earl of Mar, Gibbs secured important commissions as a church architect in London, and subsequently
as a designer of country houses for the Tory nobility. Yet
he was also patronised by the Whig Duke of Argyll. This
'universality' of appeal in Gibbs's style was reinforced by
the popularity of his immensely successful book of his
own designs, first published in 1728. This compilation
includes not only specific buildings, but also generalised
'ornaments' such as church monuments, door-cases,
chimney-pieces, cartouches, balustrades and urns.
Gibbs succeeded in giving to the world a work of dual
purpose: at once a personal manifesto of idiosyncratic
style, and a most useful pattern-book that others might
copy in remote locations. Many a country gentleman-
amateur, in Great Britain or the American colonies,
found inspiration for his own house or parish church,
to be erected with the help of a local builder. Gibbs's
St Martin-in-the-Fields (1722-26) was a hugely
influential building, and its combination of steeple

A Perspective View of St Martins Church

and classical pedimented portico became the pattern for
Georgian Anglican church-building worldwide.

JAMES GIBBS, *A Book of Architecture*, second edition (London, 1739)
A. 86. b

8.15 Bute's short-lived seaside beauty

ROBERT ADAM'S STYLE of architecture and interior decoration was
extremely influential, and pervaded
the work of many less inventive
designers. The third Earl of Bute,
the notoriously unpopular prime
minister of the earlier 1760s, was
one of Adam's important early
patrons. Subsequently, Bute
commissioned Robert Nasmith

(a little-known, probably Scottish,
architect) to execute Adam's
designs for Luton Hoo, Bedford-
shire. He then employed Nasmith
to design Highcliffe House, an
opulent cliff-top villa of remarkably
large proportions, on the Hamp-
shire coast near Christchurch.
Immensely rich, Bute was an
extravagant builder, a collector of

taste and discrimination, and a
scientist of some distinction: all
these tendencies and interests came
together at Highcliffe. Bute had
marked the site for development
when out botanising; his house was
to contain four libraries, natural history and fossil rooms, and a
laboratory. This pleasure palace *cum*
natural history research institute
had a regrettably short life of only
20 years, being demolished about
1795 due to coastal erosion. This
watercolour by Major-General John
Brown from one of his many sketch-
and note-books, which are packed
with topographical information
and minutely detailed drawings
of military interest, forms a rare
surviving contemporary record
of the building.

Brown Papers, MS. 2864, ff. 14v-15

8.16 The Rome of the North?

THE IDEA OF EDINBURGH as 'the Athens of the North' came to maturity in the early nineteenth century. But it is debatable whether Edinburgh was 'Athenian' because it resembled ancient Athens, both in topographical terms and as a city of the intellect, and therefore lent itself to the acquisition of buildings in the newly fashionable 'Greek revival' style; or simply because those fashionable buildings in the new taste of the day made it look 'Greek'. Calton Hill was thought to resemble the Athenian Acropolis and was gradually crowned with some fine Greek revival structures. The scheme for a so-called National Monument, a memorial to the Scottish dead of the French wars, resulted in a number of designs in differing tastes and scales. In the end, the archaeologically-exact C. R. Cockerell, and Edinburgh's own Greek *wunderkind* W. H. Playfair, jointly won the day with what was to be an exact replica of the Parthenon. It proved too costly for the limited funds available, leading to the branding of the fragment actually built as 'Edinburgh's Disgrace' or 'Scotland's Folly'. Archibald Elliot, in a rearguard action for Rome, had proposed this vast Pantheon-like temple, which would have been preposterous for its site, and even more impossible for the public purse. Despite much local personal support for Elliot, the prevailing mood was for a Greek rather than a Roman temple. The philhellenes won, and early nineteenth-century Edinburgh remains known as the 'Northern' or the 'Modern' Athens.

From *Report of the Proceedings of a Numerous and Respectable Meeting... with a View to the Erection of a National Monument in the Metropolis of Scotland* (Edinburgh, 1819)

LC. 3344.21

8.17 Vegetable cathedrals

FOR MOST OF THE eighteenth century, the Gothic (or 'Gothick') was a style associated with ignorance or barbarism and the terms were generally pejorative. Classicism was equated with civilisation, rationality and enlightenment; and classical taste prevailed. When, therefore, Sir James Hall, began to interest himself in the origins of gothic architecture, he was ploughing an eccentric furrow. Hall was an East Lothian baronet and a leading light of the Scottish scientific firmament – a chemist and geologist, and president of the Royal Society of Edinburgh. He believed that the gothic style had organic origins and was derived from vegetable forms: the sprouting ash used in primitive huts developed into the cluster columns, crockets and finials of sophisticated masonry buildings, and the curling of dried bark was the ultimate origin of tracery cusps. He showed logically and pictorially how massive though delicate timber structures with spreading branches forming 'natural' vaulting, with wattle and osier 'details', had become transmogrified into the stone naves, aisles, crossings, fan-vaults and window tracery of gothic buildings. Following a briefer exposition of his vegetable theories in a paper for the Royal Society of Edinburgh, Hall published a full-scale work on the subject with fine

plates by Edward Blore, 13 drawings for which are in the Library's collection (Acc. 12083). Hall even went so far as to have a wooden 'cathedral' constructed on his estate at Dunglass in experimental pursuit of his theory.

SIR JAMES HALL, *Essay on the Origin, History, and Principles of Gothic Architecture* (Edinburgh, 1813)

RB. I. 140

Science and Engineering

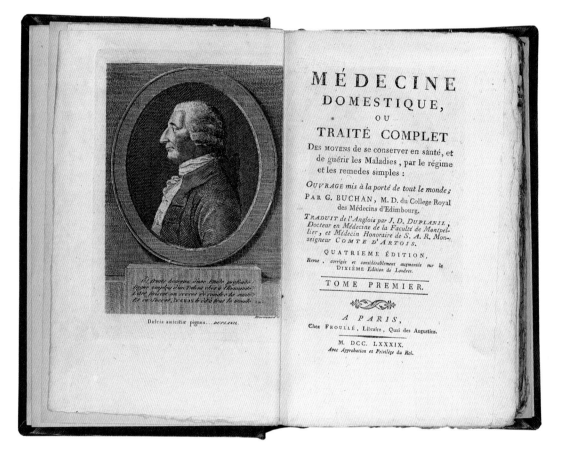

9.1 Doctor in the house

SCOTS HAVE LONG BEEN prominent in the medical sciences, and in the eighteenth century were world leaders. We tend to think of advances and ground-breaking progress in anatomy, surgery, neurology, military medicine, anaesthetics and suchlike; and we may overlook the more 'ordinary' skills of general practice, diagnostics and prescribing. Scottish publishing reflects a long tradition of progress in medicine, as indeed it does in all the sciences. Scotland's first medical book, Gilbert Skeyne's *Ane Breve Descriptioune of the Pest* appeared in 1568, and the only known copy is in the Library (H.33.b.41). William Buchan brought out his *Domestic Medicine; or, the Family Physician* in Edinburgh in 1769. A practical guide aimed at showing the layman how to prevent as well

as cure disease, it was a worldwide bestseller, with nineteen editions in the author's lifetime, and was especially popular in America. It was much translated, with a Welsh edition in 1831 and, remarkably, one in Japanese in 1817, an abridgement of a Dutch translation of 1780. The greatly expanded French edition of the fateful year 1789 unfortunately could offer no advice about the effects on bodily health of *madame la guillotine*. Buchan helped to promote the general idea of the reliable Scottish doctor; he was the Dr Cameron of his day.

G[UILLAUME] BUCHAN, *Médecine Domestique, ou Traité Complet des Moyens de Conserver en Santé, et Guérir les Maladies...*,
7 vols (Paris, 1789)
NF. 1503. f. 11

9.2 What's wrong with my horse?

Before the nineteenth century, the world was almost wholly dependent upon horse-power for most land transport. Veterinary medicine, however primitive, was therefore an important science; the farrier's business was a significant one and if no professional was to hand, the tradesman, industrialist or gentleman needed access to a modicum of basic equine knowledge. This Sir William Hope of Kirkliston set out to provide in 1696, with his translation of the text-book of the French royal riding academy. Hope, lieutenant governor of Edinburgh Castle,

supplied additional material compiled from a variety of contemporary equestrian manuals. The result was a comprehensive hand- (or hoof-) book on horse-care, the equivalent of a car main-tenance-manual. It has a splendidly imaginative title-page by George Scougall, followed by this fascinating chart of horse-problems, with a key to where in the text to find the relevant information.

Jacques de Solleysel, *The Parfait Mareschal, or Compleat Farrier*, translated by Sir William Hope (Edinburgh, 1696)

Ferg. 204

Deux géologues rapportant à Mrs Ellice, un petit echantillon des Montagnes moutonnées découvertes en 1860, entre Glenquoich et Lochhourne
[en gaelique : Sbchhgdh]

9.3 Geologists surveyed

IT WOULD BE INVIDIOUS, and doubtless wildly inaccurate and superficial, to say that one science more than any other was especially and specifically 'Scottish'; but geology must be a prime candidate for any such flawed competition. In the later eighteenth century, James Hutton advanced theories that provoked a revolution in thinking about the concept of 'deep time'. In a famous phrase he asserted that he could detect, in the geological evidence for a cycle of continuous creation, 'no vestige of a beginning… no prospect of an end'. Among the procession of distinguished nineteenth-century pioneers of Scottish geology were Sir Roderick Murchison and Sir Archibald Geikie. Both are shown in this caricature by the French novelist and dramatist Prosper Mérimée. Mérimée was staying with his friend, the businessman and politician Edward Ellice, at his shooting lodge at Glenquoich, where the

Ellices entertained the Victorian political and social establishment – as the family papers and visitors' books in the Library record (cf. 13.11-12, 14.5). Murchison with his hammer, and Geikie with a boulder, come in from their researches in the locality, bringing their scientific findings as tribute to Mrs Ellice. Mérimée cannot resist a French pun: the geological specimen comes from the '*Montagnes moutonnées*', that is 'glaciated', a term derived from 'sheep' (*mouton*), of which a flock is shown approaching. Nor can Archibald Geikie's specific role in this caricature have been accidental. Murchison was the first director of the British Geological Survey and Geikie was his devoted assistant. The younger, stone-carrying Scotsman had recently published a popular book that was to be the first of many seminal works; it was entitled *The Story of a Boulder*.
Ellice Papers, MS. 15174, no. 76

Scots gardeners and nurserymen dominated the horticultural and botanical world of eighteenth-century Britain and much of Europe besides. A contemporary garden writer called them 'the northern lads who have invaded the southern provinces'. The literature of the subject was likewise overshadowed by the work of Scotsmen, notably Philip Miller with his highly influential *Gardeners Dictionary*, in its several incarnations. This great compendium is shown in the splendid, expensively showy and unusually large-scale trade-card of Henry Scott, dating from 1754. Miller's book is propped against the potted pineapple plant by Scott's right leg. In a delightfully absurd fantasy, classical gods and personifications sample Scott's luscious produce in his nursery at Weybridge, Surrey, in juxtaposition with such thoroughly modern devices as thermometers and hot-houses. Scott had set up there after serving Lord Burlington at Chiswick; pineapples were his speciality. This copy of the trade-card (measuring twelve inches by nine, drawn to Scott's design by Samuel Wale and engraved by François Vivares) has in manuscript an advertising puff that was subsequently engraved on later versions: 'Knowledge and Labour assisted by the four Elements presenting the Gardener with a Cornucopia of Fruits which are the Produce of the Hottest Climates'.

K. 117. c. 2 (16)

9.5 **Tales of heads**

The pseudo-science of phrenology, or 'craniology', captured the imagination of many in the nineteenth century, and none more so than the Edinburgh lawyer George Combe. The extensive correspondence, notes and papers which Combe and his circle accumulated on this subject were presented to the Library in 1950: they occupy 313 volumes. Combe's comprehensive library of phrenological literature had been bequeathed to the Advocates in the late 1860s. These resources make Edinburgh a world centre for research into the remarkable phenomenon of phrenology. Contemporaries did not always see the 'science' as worthy of credence; Walter Scott wrote acidly of this '*ology* of the present day' as 'superstitious nonsense', and denigrated it as '… Scullology, I forget its learned name'. Many shared his view; but many also were obsessed by this new method of measuring character and mental faculties by physical study of the cranium. J.G. Lockhart flirted with 'cranioscopical mania' and 'the calm consideration of skulls and faces', but suspected that 'the suspicion or reproach of quackery' was never far away.

Among Combe's books was this French work which examines facial and physical 'types' and gestures, in a series of amusing plates; in this one, boys mimic their elders' every gesture.

Hippolyte Bruyères, *La Phrénologie. Le Geste et la Physionomie* (Paris, 1848)

Combe. 1.1.12

9.6 The colossus of roads

THE SCOTTISH ENGINEER – civil, mechanical or industrial – is as much a national stereotype as the Scottish doctor, and as much a byword for reliability. No ship in the world, it once seemed, lacked a Mactavish in the engine-room, and even Star Trek's *Enterprise* has 'Scotty' as its engineer. Civil engineering is another of the great 'Scottish' sciences. The papers of several of these titans are in the Library. This portrait of Thomas Telford, called 'the Colossus of Roads' (though he is best known for his bridges, aqueducts and canals and purely architectural work), appears as frontispiece to the vast *Atlas* which supplements his autobiography, edited by John Rickman in 1838. The volume contains 83 plates of Telford's numerous works and thus furnishes a complete record 'illustrative of his professional labours'. In the background

appears one of Telford's most magnificent achievements, the Pontcysyllte aqueduct which carries the Llangollen canal across the Dee valley in north Wales, a structure that remains a wonder of world engineering. In the front is one of Telford's many highland Scottish bridges, serving to remind us of his role in opening up the north. On the table are drawings of the Cartland Crags Bridge carrying the Carluke road over the Mouse Water in Lanarkshire (1821-22): this can be discerned from examination of what are evidently sections of piers for this bold construction. The original portrait by Samuel Lane hangs in the Institution of Civil Engineers, of which Telford was first president.

Atlas to the Life of Thomas Telford, Civil Engineer... (London, 1838)
FB. el. 116

9.7 London Bridge is going up!

JOHN RENNIE the elder began his career as a millwright and general mechanical engineer, but subsequently turned to the work on docks, harbours and bridges that made him famous. All his bridges, like those of his senior contemporary Thomas Telford, can be appreciated as fine works of architecture as well as superb examples of the engineer's art. Rennie took up the challenge of bridging the Thames on three occasions, and gave London the Strand (later renamed Waterloo) Bridge, Southwark Bridge and, lastly, London Bridge. Telford had designed a single-span cast iron bridge for this site but Rennie's five-arch masonry bridge was preferred. Rennie died in 1821. His son John oversaw its construction, to his father's design, and it was opened by King William IV in 1831, when young Rennie was knighted, giving a further fillip to the rising professional status of the civil engineer in Great Britain. Shown here is a souvenir of the occasion, preserved in the Rennie Papers. This collection was the first of the great engineering archives to be acquired (in 1970) by the Library. London Bridge was demolished just before this time, and was being reconstructed at Lake Havasu City, Arizona, at the moment the papers of its designer and builder were being bought for Edinburgh; so all was not lost to Britain.

Rennie Papers, MS. 19772, f. 122

9.8 Lighthouse luxury

THE STEVENSON FAMILY will be forever associated with the business of lighthouse building. Robert Stevenson also built roads, harbours and bridges in a career rather similar to those of Telford and John Rennie the elder; but he found a specialist niche in the design and construction of lighthouses for the Commissioners of Northern Lights. First, and possibly most famous of all his works, was the Bell Rock Light; but many others followed. The Stevenson Papers in the Library (Acc. 10706), a large and highly important collection, are rich in manuscript and engraved plans,

elevations and sections of these remarkable constructions. But a much more unusual view of the Bell Rock Light, indeed of its interior, is furnished by this watercolour by the novelist R.M. Ballantyne, who had spent time on the Bell Rock while researching a book, eventually published as *The Lighthouse* (1865). Ballantyne had also gone to dry out; remarkably frank letters to his sister-in-law, acquired with this sketch, describe his battle with the bottle in his sea-girt, wave-lashed eyrie. They also describe life in the lighthouse, such as Sunday morning service conducted in the library by the chief keeper. This fascinating record shows that the keepers' accommodation was not unduly spartan, with its furniture made to fit the curvature of tower and dome (which had a coffered ceiling), busts, paintings, brightly patterned carpets, and a tripod table with sea-monster legs.

Acc. 11962

Literature 10

10.1 A nation's literature saved

IN 1568 GEORGE BANNATYNE, an Edinburgh merchant, retired to the country to escape the plague then ravaging the city ('in tyme of pest'). He occupied himself in transcribing a collection of all the Scottish poetry he knew, preserving much that might have been lost: his compilation includes otherwise unrecorded work by the great 'makars' of the fifteenth and sixteenth centuries, for example Robert Henryson, William Dunbar, Gavin Douglas, Sir David Lindsay, Alexander Montgomerie, and by many lesser writers of verse. A later admirer of Bannatyne's work described the compilation as 'Ane most Godlie, mirrie, and lustie Rapsodie, maide by sundrie learned Scots Poets'. Sir Walter Scott, later still, described the work done by Bannatyne 'in the tyme of his youth' as raising him from 'an humble copyist to a national benefactor'. The Bannatyne Manuscript was presented to the Advocates' Library in 1772 by the Earl of Hyndford, becoming, again in Scott's words, 'public property' – a very interesting view of the 'national' status of what was still technically a private institution. Allan Ramsay had earlier borrowed the manuscript, and based upon it his own selection of ballads and verses published as *The Ever Green* (1724). In characteristically confident manner, Ramsay had inscribed on the precious manuscript a scrawling note expressing the debt he had incurred. The manuscript, bound in two volumes, was out of the Library for repair in February 1823, when the premises of the bookbinder entrusted with the work were destroyed by fire. The invaluable volumes were rescued, just as Bannatyne had saved the country's literature 255 years previously.

Adv. MS. 1.1.6

The
Gentle Shepherd
a
Scots
Pastorall Comedy

By

Allan Ramsay

Written in the years 1724 & 1725 at the 40th of his age

This is the Originall Manuscript from which
the Coppys were Printed; Presented to my Patroness
March 2d 1737 — after my having seen reprinted Six
Editions of it a thousand each time besides two in London
one in Dublin & one in Glasgow — and be it kend to
you Curious posterity, that the performance has received the
universall approbation as I hope it will from you
Thousands of years hence

N.B. The additional Songs were added to the
fourth Edition about the year 1782 by the author

10.2 **The universal approbation of posterity**

THE CHARACTER OF Allan Ramsay was liberally endowed with a vanity, and a consciousness of reputation, almost charming in their innocence. In completing one of the two surviving manuscripts of his pastoral comedy *The Gentle Shepherd* in 1725, he was moved to add a whimsical note to the title-page: 'And be it kend to You, Curious Posterity, that the performance has received the universall approbation as I hope it will, from You, Thousands of years hence.' In this he is unlikely to be right; but the drama, a work of immense contemporary popularity, went through innumerable editions and remained in his compatriots' affections, as a relatively faithful portrait of Lowland country life, for at least a century and a half thereafter. Burns was a great admirer of the work, particularly in the fine edition published by the Foulis brothers of Glasgow in 1788 (the first Scottish publishing house to enjoy a European reputation for excellence), with its delightful aquatint plates by David Allan. The provenance of this manuscript, which preserves the final version of the work before it was revised by its author in 1729 and transformed into a ballad opera, is interesting. Ramsay presented it to Susanna, Countess of Eglinton, in 1737. She, as an old woman, gave it to James Boswell. It was sold in the Auchinleck sale in 1893, and it subsequently entered the Charles R. Cowie Collection of manuscripts of Burns, Scott and other Scottish writers, which passed to the Library in 1964.

MS. 15972

10.3 'By far my elder brother in the muse'

ROBERT FERGUSSON, who died in tragic circumstances at the age of 24, forms a link between Allan Ramsay and Robert Burns in the tradition of poets who chose to express their deepest and most affecting thoughts in Scots. The Library's collection of the Cape Club records (MSS. 2000-45) preserves Fergusson's petition of admission to this debating society, which expressed much of the convivial life of the Edinburgh that Fergusson loved and immortalised in his poems, notably his 'Auld Reekie' of 1773. He had published work in Thomas Ruddiman's *Weekly Magazine, or Edinburgh Amusement* in 1772 and 1773. Ruddiman, nephew of Thomas Ruddiman, the

great Advocates' Librarian, also issued a volume of the poet's best work in 1773. The copy shown here bears Fergusson's autograph dedication, in verse, to his friend the shoemaker (or 'souter') and poetaster Gavin Wilson, a man archly described as 'leather tormentor' and who also made prosthetic limbs. Burns, Fergusson's devoted admirer and a man who himself understood adversity, inscribed his own copy of this collection with the couplet: 'My elder brother in misfortune / By far my elder brother in the muse.' Burns later commissioned and paid for a headstone over Fergusson's unmarked, pauper's grave in the Canongate kirkyard.

ROBERT FERGUSSON, *Poems*
(Edinburgh, 1773)
L. C. 124

10.4 True old-style Caledonian feelings

ALL THE WORLD KNOWS Robert Burns as a poet; the Library holds many of his manuscript poems, most notably his own collection of some of his best work, the Glenriddell Manuscripts (MSS. 86-87). But Burns was also a songwriter of genius, and a collector and adapter of the ballads and folksongs of his country. He was, furthermore, a prolific and important letter-writer, many of these epistles being carefully crafted in the most elegant English of the day, and written with an eye to posterity. A selection of his letters forms part of the Glenriddell Manuscripts. Song-collecting and writing are the subject of this short but significant letter of 1787 to William Tytler of Woodhouselee; Burns indicates

that the song-culture of Scotland had once been almost entirely ignored and uncared for. He alludes to the possibility that old songs might lend themselves to adaptation; and though he protests that he holds it as 'sacriledge' to 'add any thing of my own to help out the shatter'd wrecks of these venerable old compositions', he often did just that. He hopes that Tytler will have his 'true old-style Caledonian feelings' stirred by the songs he sends. Tytler was interested in early Scottish poetry and had helped James Johnson with his *Scots Musical Museum*, to which Burns was a major contributor of songs. He also encouraged George Thomson with his later *Select Scottish Airs*, this too containing much work by Burns.

Watson Collection
MS. 586, no, 1129 (f. 24)

10.5 An electric shock of delight

WALTER SCOTT, perceiving that his star as an astoundingly successful author of narrative poetry was being eclipsed by that of Byron, suddenly emerged as a writer of prose fiction with *Waverley* in 1814. The rest is history – or, in this case, one historical novel after another, in a cascade that continued unabated until 1832, when Scott could write no more. *Waverley* and its successors served to make Scotland and everything 'Scotch' fashionable and world-famous. Writing of the effect of that first novel, Henry Cockburn hit on a striking metaphor: Edinburgh, he remembered, had been transfixed by 'an electric shock of delight'. Scott maintained his incognito for years after the secret was an open one, probably believing that it added to the mystique of authorship and

was thus a shrewd commercial marketing ploy. Further, it seemed more gentlemanly that an advocate and sheriff should not be known to write fiction. And he simply enjoyed playing a game with his public, one made more complex still by his use of many aliases, through prefaces and introductions by others than the purported writer, and so on. The manuscript of *Waverley* was presented to the Advocates' Library in 1850. The donor, James Hall (cf.7.8), could not have known that this single act of generosity would lead to the formation, over the next 160 years, of what is arguably the finest collection in any library in the world of a great writer's literary manuscripts, correspondence and papers. Adv. MS. 1. 1. 0.

10.6 **Two people unhappy**

SAMUEL BUTLER waspishly observed that it was good of God to let Mr and Mrs Carlyle marry each other, because that way only *two* people had been made unhappy. It is true that the 'Sage of Chelsea' was, and remains, an acquired taste, in both character and literary style, but it seems a little hard on long-suffering Jane Welsh Carlyle, who had so much to endure from her husband's irascibility, his long absences from home, and his devotion to a number of aristocratic, married ladies. 'I too am here…', Jane Carlyle once remonstrated with her husband when he was being unreasonable; and indeed, over the years, she has emerged from her husband's shadow as one the great letter-writers and diarists of her age. Her private journals record a life of tortured and repressed feelings. Reading this notebook only after her death, her chastened widower added his own comments and reminiscences of his late wife. The Library is the world centre of Carlyle studies, with vast collections of correspondence of the Carlyles and their circle, together with literary manuscripts and other papers. A particularly evocative letter is that from Carlyle to his publisher, explaining that the completed manuscript of his history of the French revolution had just been burned in error by John Stuart Mill's maid, a circumstance that Carlyle accepted with remarkable fortitude, and which we might well regard as worthy of his own doctrine of 'Hero Worship' (Acc. 6430). Shown here is a witty take on 'Hero Worship', in the form of a drawing by Elizabeth Paulet of a visiting literary lion-hunter viewing a pair of Carlyle's trousers, while the owner sits smoking in his garden beyond.

Carlyle Collection, MS. 533, MS. 603, f. 201

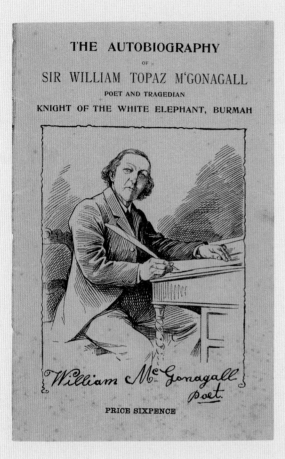

THE AUTOBIOGRAPHY
OF
SIR WILLIAM TOPAZ M'GONAGALL
POET AND TRAGEDIAN
KNIGHT OF THE WHITE ELEPHANT, BURMAH

William Mc Gonagall
Poet.

PRICE SIXPENCE

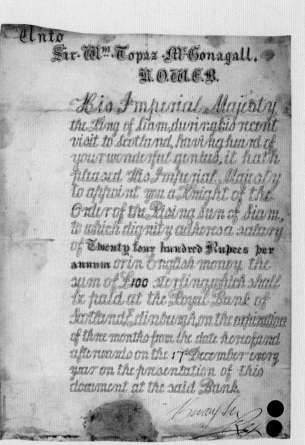

10.7 The white elephant of literature

WILLIAM McGONAGALL's 'poetic' output was as large as it was bad. There was nothing too prosaic to merit his bathetic tribute, and no character of the later Victorian state or empire, no disaster, battle, illness or death, that failed to elicit from him a truly terrible commemorative or celebratory ode. Students of the university of Edinburgh mockingly invested him, in 1894, with an honour purportedly the gift of the king of Burma. McGonagall took this to his heart, and ever afterwards called himself 'Sir William Topaz McGonagall, Knight of the White Elephant'. His self-awarded literary epithet was 'Poet and Tragedian'. The Library holds a substantial collection of his printed ballads, which he invariably signed or otherwise inscribed (often with dedications to prominent individuals) to add dignity and thus vicarious approbation. A copy of his pamphlet autobiography is shown here, together with a spurious document which purports to confer on him a pension (payable on the Royal Bank of Scotland: McGonagall did not live long enough to see another joke there) from the king of Siam, by whom he had also been invested with a further order, 'the Rising Sun'. This spoof does not seem to have been noted by McGonagall biographers.

L. C. Fol. 71/ 1 and 2

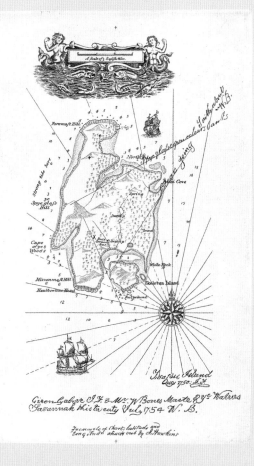

10.8 'Harbours that pleased me like sonnets'

'I am told', wrote Robert Louis Stevenson, 'that there are people who do not care for maps, and find it hard to believe… here is an inexhaustible fund of interest for any man with eyes to see, or tuppenceworth of imagination to understand with'. He was describing the origin of *Treasure Island*, which began with a map of an island, drawn (according to their varying accounts) by RLS himself or by his stepson Lloyd Osbourne. The map, with its 'harbours that pleased me like sonnets', and the exciting story that sprang from it, developed into a tale originally entitled 'The Sea Cook'; this was changed by a shrewd publisher. Stevenson had loved islands since an early voy-age in the yacht of the Commissioners of Northern Lights. The original map was lost in the press and RLS was obliged to redraw it, based upon his text – reversing the order of the book's creation. He felt, however, that it lacked the spontaneity of the original, which had inspired so much, but in his introduction he did pay the most generous and eloquent tribute to the importance and inspiration of maps in general, and of maps in fiction in particular. Shown here is the original copperplate, engraved by the cartographers Bartholomew, with a pull.

Bartholomew Archive, Acc. 10222/Copperplates/Box 43
Bartholomew Archive, Acc. 10222/Business Archive/99

10.9 'The plan of every house plotted on paper'

IN HIS ACCOUNT of the genesis of *Treasure Island*, Stevenson advocated the importance of a map to a writer of fiction, for an author 'must know his countryside whether real or imaginary, like his hand… With an almanac, and the map of the country and the plan of every house either actually plotted on paper or clearly and immediately apprehended in the mind, a man may hope to avoid some of the grossest possible blunders.' He upbraided himself for having made some blunders himself, but criticised Scott for having made even more spectacular ones. James Leslie Mitchell (who wrote as Lewis Grassic Gibbon) might have had Stevenson's advice in mind when he drew this plan of the streets and buildings of Segget. This was the town in the Mearns to which, in the novel *Cloud Howe* (the second book of the *Scots Quair* trilogy), Chris Guthrie moves, and where she becomes the wife of the minister. The higgledy-piggledy town plan shows a place very different from the ordered world of Welwyn Garden City in Hertfordshire, where Mitchell was living when he wrote the novel. The plan of Segget features in a notebook forming part of Mitchell's papers, acquired in 1981. Mitchell's is one of many collections of modern Scottish authors, actively acquired by the Library from the 1960s onwards. These make it a major research centre for twentieth-century and contemporary literary studies.

MS. 26041

10.10 Whaur extremes meet: the Caledonian antisyzygy

A Drunk Man Looks at the Thistle (1926), by Christopher Murray Grieve (who wrote as Hugh MacDiarmid), contributed to Scottish literature one of its greatest twentieth-century achievements. The work typifies the contradictions, dualism, and tension between opposites that MacDiarmid and others saw as inherent in the Scots character and its literary, emotional and spiritual expression. A drunk man lies in the moonlight before a huge thistle, which metamorphoses into many things symbolic of the contradictions and contrasts of Scotland, and indeed of the human condition. His speculations range far and wide on eternal questions of meaning and existence. This woodcut by Frans Masereel, a Belgian artist of European significance, appears opposite a page of text in which MacDiarmid mocks 'tartanry', the universality of the 'Burns supper' tradition, London Scots, and the very image of Scotland. It illustrates a fine limited edition produced only nine years before the author's death. Hand-printed at the Officina Bodoni in Verona on paper made in Amalfi, the copies were signed by author, printer and illustrator, and the edition was published in Scotland by

Kulgin Duval and Colin Hamilton. They subsequently acquired the very extensive MacDiarmid papers and sold them to the Library, where they much enhanced the holdings of twentieth-century Scottish literary and 'Scottish renaissance' material. Many other such literary archives have followed.

HUGH MACDIARMID, *A Drunk Man Looks at the Thistle* (Falkland, 1969)

FB. m. 34

10.11 Tunes of over-confidence

OF THE HALF DOZEN novels James Kennaway published before his death in a car accident at the age of 40, *Tunes of Glory* (1956) will be longest remembered. This is largely on account of the powerful film of 1960, starring Alec Guinness and John Mills as two army officers of very different social and military backgrounds and experiences. Kennaway himself wrote the screenplay. The story of tension in the mess of a post-war Scottish regiment draws on Kennaway's own experience of National Service in the Cameron Highlanders. During this time Kennaway, brashly cocky and on leave in St Albans, wrote in verse to George Bernard Shaw, the grand old man of English letters who lived nearby at Ayot St Lawrence, inviting himself to interview Shaw and (he hoped) to tea. Shaw refused both, in a verse matching Kennaway's own entreaty, and inscribed and returned on Kennaway's own letter-card. Conveniently, one writes in blue ink, the other in red.

Acc. 5696/ Box 1, no 4

10.12 Miss Muriel Spark before her prime

THE ENORMOUS ARCHIVE of Dame Muriel Spark, at the time of her death the unquestioned *doyenne* of Scottish literature, has been coming to the Library in stages over many years, home from Tuscany, where Spark had latterly lived, to the city of her birth. Here she was educated, at James Gillespie's High School, adjoining Bruntsfield Links, prototype of the Marcia Blaine School where the redoubtable Miss Jean Brodie taught 'in her prime'. Many US libraries would have given much to acquire this archive, just as an American publisher tried to persuade Muriel Spark to offer them her eventual autobiography. In the Spark Papers (Acc.10607/ 85) is an intriguing letter of 1988 from Jacqueline Kennedy Onassis, urging Spark to write her life for Doubleday, the New York house for which 'Jackie O.' acted as a roving social talent-scout *cum* commissioning editor. Spark eventually published her autobiography, *Curriculum Vitae*, in 1992, with Constable of London. The second of a series of notebooks containing a first draft of this work is entitled 'The School on the Links', and opens with a discussion of the distinctive Edinburgh educational tradition of charitable institutions established for children of the lower middle classes or trades. Spark always wrote in longhand, in Bothwell spiral jotters, which she had sent out to S. Giovanni in Oliveto, Civitella della Chiana, from James Thin, bookseller and stationer in Edinburgh.

Acc. 10989/ 255

10.13 **Word and image**

ALL ALASDAIR GRAY's productions are 'total' works of art, from their intellectual content – remarkable and ground-breaking – to their typography and illustration, their covers and their dust-jackets, all of these self-designed. Even the filing boxes in which his papers are stored in the Library have about them a quality of art, as Gray has arranged and listed much of his archive himself, and the files are labelled in his idiosyncratic handwriting. *Lanark. A Life in Four Books* (1981) established Gray as a major force on the literary and artistic scene. His novel had been many years in the making. 'Work as if you live in the early days of a better nation' is a saying by, or at any rate adopted by, Gray as a kind of life-motto: it has since been enshrined among the apophthegms engraved on the walls of the new Scottish Parliament building. Shown here is the original artwork for a divisional title-page of *Lanark.* The figure of a giant, wielding sword and crosier, is derived from that by Abraham Bosse which forms the upper part of the allegorical image ornamenting the title-page of Thomas Hobbes's *Leviathan* of 1651. Gray's giant rises over a brilliantly conceived bird's-eye prospect of central Scotland, extending from Arran and the Clyde estuary, with the nuclear submarines on the Gare Loch, to the oil-rig be-starred North Sea. Gray himself sits at the foot, counterpart to the giant. This 'view map' makes it own contribution to the record of the image of Scotland as land of mountain and flood (cf.1.1).

Acc. 10119/ 6

Printing and Publishing 11

11.1 Smellie's printing house

THE DETAIL IN THIS watercolour by Walter Dunn, a foreman printer for the great William Smellie, is interesting and instructive for its illustration of life and work in a celebrated print shop. At the right, men work the presses. The press-man on the extreme right raises the frisket which secures the paper to the tympan so that the whole, resting on the bed of type, may be slid beneath the platen, on which pressure is exerted by means of screw and lever to produce the printed sheet. Struts to the ceiling steady the entire hand-press machinery.

At the left, a compositor stands before the type, arranged by sizes and fonts, in its cases, 'upper' and 'lower' – terms we still use without thinking of their original meaning. Apprentices scurry between the two halves of the room. The hats of the workforce hang on pegs along the wall. Dunn included this sketch, dated 1807, in an unusual album he compiled in 1827. It has a typeset title-page and other printed elements, but contains many original drawings, watercolours and manuscript pieces.
RB. s. 612

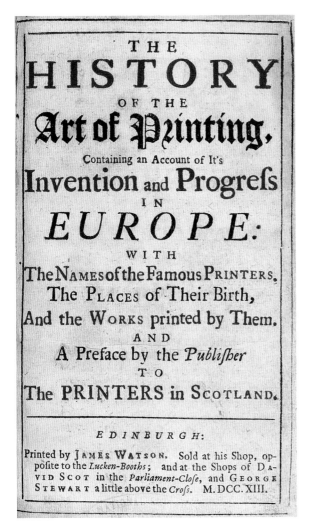

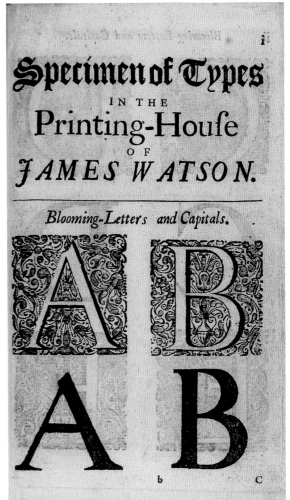

11.2 The imprint of a people

PRINTING CAME LATE to Scotland, in 1508, but the nation more than compensated for this in succeeding centuries and has long occupied a distinguished place, out of proportion to its size or population, in the history of the printing trade and in publishing. These industries were significant in the Scottish economy until the latter part of the twentieth century. If the glory days are now past, the legacy can be studied in the great historical archives of printing and publishing accumulated by the Library over many years of active collecting. The 500th anniversary of printing in Scotland (which can be dated precisely to 4 April 1508) was celebrated in 2008, and many of the early productions of the sixteenth and early seventeenth centuries have been duly re-examined, rehearsed and celebrated. These include the work of Andrew Myllar and Walter Chepman, Thomas Davidson, Henry Charteris,

Thomas Bassandyne and Alexander Arbuthnet, Andro Hart (all of Edinburgh); Robert Lekpreuik in St Andrews; and the earliest patrons such as King James IV and Bishop William Elphinstone. In the eighteenth century, Scottish printers and publishers kept pace with the intellectual advances of their countrymen in every aspect of arts, letters and science, producing work of the highest quality and elegance. Nineteenth-century Scottish printers and publishers would lead the world. James Watson's survey of past developments, in the European context, and of contemporary practice in his own shop has historical curiosity-value, even if he contrives to omit any mention of the real origins of the trade in Scotland, and the names of Chepman and Myllar.

JAMES WATSON, *The History of the Art of Printing...* (Edinburgh, 1713)
L.C. 1639

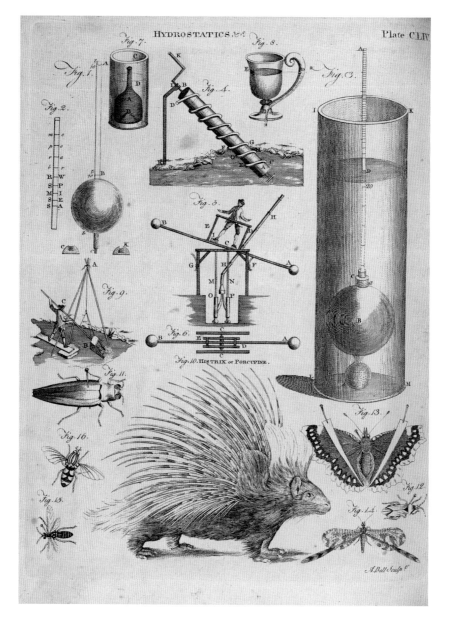

11.3 A universe of knowledge

ALTHOUGH IT IS Wikipedia that we all use daily (with circumspection), and though Diderot and D'Alembert's great *L'Encyclopédie* predates it, the *Encyclopaedia Britannica* still remains a matchless source of knowledge, deriving ultimately from the ideals of the Enlightenment. It was first published in Edinburgh in parts, between 1768 and 1771, by a 'Society of Gentlemen in Scotland' under the editorship of William Smellie, who supplied the text himself. Smellie was also a notable printer in his own right, producing many of the great Enlightenment titles. Andrew Bell was joint publisher and proprietor with Colin Macfarquhar. Bell himself engraved the plates, which grew in number and complexity as the encyclopaedia expanded through its various editions.

James Tytler, eccentric and balloonist, undertook the second edition (1777-84), like Smellie furnishing most of the contents himself; these he allegedly wrote on an upturned washtub in his cottage lodging at Duddingston village on the edge of Edinburgh. His edition appeared in parts and was then re-issued in ten volumes quarto from 1778. This plate from the second edition demonstrates the *Encyclopaedia*'s concern with embracing the universe of knowledge: engravings illustrating the machinery of hydrostatics keep company with those of beetles, butterflies and a rather appealing porcupine.

Encyclopaedia Britannica, second edition (1778-83), vol. 5 (Edinburgh, 1780)

EB. 2

11.4   **An author checks his proofs**

WILLIAM COMBE's splendid and wickedly clever satire on the picturesque tour of the portly divine, Dr Paul Prosody, through Scotland (cf. 13.1), followed the success of Combe's three volumes of Dr Syntax's tours in England. It concludes with the hero watching his book of Scottish travels being printed after his return to London. Prosody stands with his friend Dr Factobend beside a press, from which the printed sheets are taken and hung up to dry. A man wields his dabbers to apply ink to the surface of the type. Prosody, anxious to see his book in print, urges haste, and pays handsomely to slake the sweating printers' thirst with beer. In Combe's witty text, a perfect foil for the delightful illustrations, the compositor is made to assure Prosody that Dr Syntax himself, established 'author' though he is, offers no competition in terms of likely sales and probable popularity. Thus the tyro author watches in excitement as the printed sheets come off the press, 'Until the Doctor, (some crowns minus) / Beheld, with transport, the word – *Finis*'.

[WILLIAM COMBE] *The Tour of Doctor Prosody, in Search of the Antique and Picturesque, through Scotland* (London, 1821) Hall. 151.d

11.5 Oxford dons reading *The Edinburgh Review*

The Edinburgh Review, founded in 1802 by a group led by Francis Jeffrey, set new standards in literary criticism and attracted a brilliant group of writers espousing Whig ideas. Tory Oxford cannot have been disposed to enjoy the 'Blue and Yellow', as it was known from the (Whig) colours of its wrappers. John Gibson Lockhart, an accomplished caricaturist as acerbic with brush as with his journalistic pen (cf. 2.9), drew this scene in 1810. Lockhart had gone up to Balliol as a Snell Exhibitioner from Glasgow two years before. Oxford was then – as this *tableau vivant* shows – in the twilight of its long age of 'port and prejudice'.

This drawing hardly bears out Lord Cockburn's comment, in his *Life of Lord Jeffrey* (1852), about the 'electrical' effect of the periodical upon literary and polite society. (The corrected proofs of the *Life of Jeffrey* are in the Library, MS. 345.) He likened the *Edinburgh* to a 'pillar of fire', recalling that 'its periodical appearance was looked for as that of the great exponent of what people should think on matters of taste and policy. No British journal had ever held such sway over the public mind. Nor had any one ever approached it in extent of circulation.' Acc. 11480

11.6 The honours of print and pay

FROM ITS INCEPTION in 1817 *Blackwood's Magazine*, established as a Tory rival to *The Edinburgh Review*, attracted some of the best literary talent of the day. The vast Blackwood archive (acquired by the Library between the 1940s and the 1980s) provides a remarkable conspectus of author-publisher relations over nearly two centuries. The correspondence between George Henry Lewes, Mary Ann Evans and editor John Blackwood offers one example of the process of discovering talent and establishing successful authorship. Lewes sent Blackwood a story purportedly by an elderly, diffident clergyman, but actually by his inamorata, Mary Ann Evans. After much interchange of letters, the story was accepted and its author pronounced by Blackwood 'worthy of the honours of print and pay'. Slowly the

truth came out: the writer was a woman, her 'agent' was actually her lover, and this fresh literary talent, wishing to preserve 'the iron mask of [her] incognito', was to adopt a *nom de plume* shortly to become world-famous. Various stages of subterfuge ensued. On the one hand, Blackwood, when he was able to write directly to the author, and still presuming the mysterious writer to be male, addressed 'The Author of Amos Barton' successively as 'Dear Sir', 'My Dear Sir', 'Dear Amos', etc., in increasing familiarity. On the other, Mary Ann Evans (in the letter part of which is shown here), writing for the first time with her pseudonym 'George Eliot', praises Blackwood for his gentle nurture of emerging talent in his role as 'best & most sympathizing of editors'.

Blackwood Papers, MS. 4123, f. 51v.

11.7 The fortunes of author and publisher

IN 1816 WILLIAM BLACKWOOD was in London on business, and his letters to his wife are rich in information about the world of publishing and bookselling. Here he describes how he had been with John Murray when Murray received a new manuscript from Lord Byron: this was the third canto of *Childe Harold's Pilgrimage*, the first two cantos of which had already made a reputation and a fortune for both Byron and Murray. Blackwood described Murray as 'quite in the clouds just now and with good reason… It [Byron's poem] is most wonderful, and the few who have seen it … think it far exceeds any thing he has yet done. He has paid in 1500 guineas to Lord Byron's banker. Lord B. did not expect more than 500 or 600. Murray will make thousands of it – what a fortunate man he is.' This letter neatly links the two publishing houses of Mur-

ray and Blackwood. The archives of the latter have long been in the Library. The fabulous John Murray Archive was acquired in 2006 for the unprecedentedly large sum of over £31 million. No more important publishing archive exists; it sheds light on almost every field of human endeavour over three centuries. It also fits seamlessly with the Library's existing collections of publishing firms and of individual authors and in so many ways has come 'home'. The letter shown here was bought in 2003 as part of a purchase at auction of a small group of Blackwood correspondence. The material had previously been on temporary deposit in 1979; it is pleasing to be able to return permanently to the Library's collections something which had in the interim disappeared from sight.

Acc. 12243

11.8 Around the world in eighty Murrays

The firm of John Murray established a reputation as a leading publisher of books on travel and exploration, as well as of works on archaeology, art and the natural and physical sciences. All these interests coalesce in the great series of 'Handbooks for Travellers', launched by the third John Murray in 1836, after his own extensive travels in Europe had made him aware of the need for up-to-date and informative guidebooks. These famous 'Red' guidebooks became standard equipment for travellers in Britain, Europe and beyond. John Murray III, who had become head of the firm in 1843, had good Scottish connections, through both his Scottish mother and his Edinburgh university education. The *Handbook for Travellers in Scotland* was his own work, and his personal effort to keep the book up to date is demonstrated by this marked-up copy for the third edition. It is heavily annotated throughout with extensive textual revisions incorporating the latest information. The account of Glencoe refers to the original manuscript order for the massacre in 1692 (an iconic document that would later enter the Library's collection in 1925 as the gift of J. Ramsay Macdonald, Adv. MS. 23.6.24). In emulation of Murray's example – Murray called it plagiarism – the rival German publisher Karl Baedeker produced his equally celebrated guidebooks; the Luftwaffe in the Second World War used these to direct its series of so-called 'Baedeker raids' on UK targets, but there is no evidence that the RAF ever launched 'Murray raids' on Germany.

John Murray Archive, MS. 42500

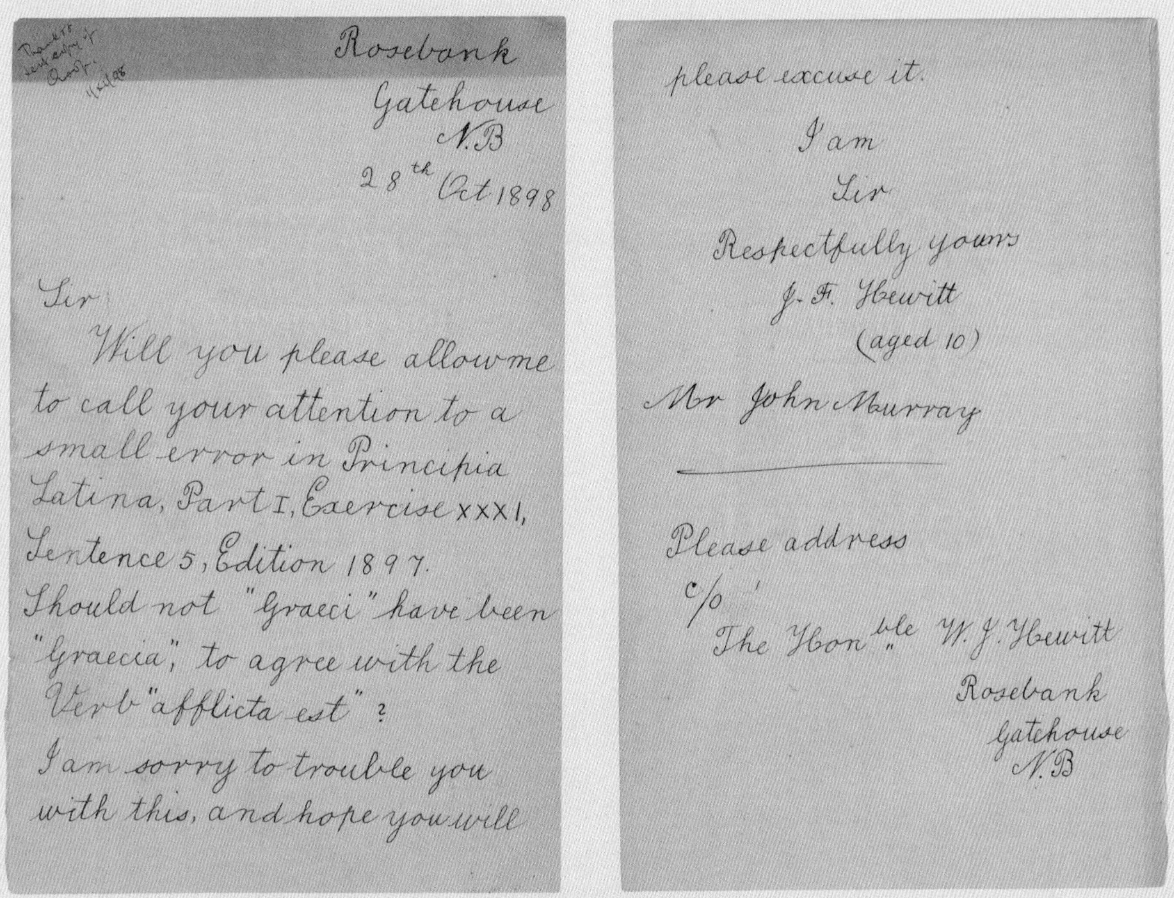

Rosebank
Gatehouse
N.B
28th Oct 1898

Sir

Will you please allow me to call your attention to a small error in *Principia Latina*, Part I, Exercise XXXI, Sentence 5, Edition 1897. Should not "Graeci" have been "Graecia", to agree with the Verb "afflicta est"? I am sorry to trouble you with this, and hope you will

please excuse it.

I am
Sir
Respectfully yours
J. F. Hewitt
(aged 10)

Mr John Murray

———

Please address
c/o
The Hon.ble W. J. Hewitt
Rosebank
Gatehouse
N.B

11.9 A precocious but doomed Murray reader

A MINOR BUT TOUCHING little find in the vastness of the John Murray Archive, so full of great names of literature and learning, is this letter from a ten-year-old schoolboy. Master James Francis Hewitt has spotted a mistake in Murray's *Principia Latina* and (without his father's knowledge) writes to the head of the firm, John Murray IV, to point this out – which he does surely, but with due measure of respectful diffidence. Evidently entertained, the publisher sent the boy a copy of Murray's edition of Aesop's *Fables*. Thanking him, James confessed that it was more his teacher's observation of the error than his own that had prompted his letter. In a further display of candour he explained that an extra copy of the presentation volume had just arrived, which he would return. But all the pedantry and honesty in the world could not hold up the march of history, and there is a sobering footnote to this tale. The young scholar of 1898, a nephew of the sixth Viscount Lifford, was killed in action on 26 October 1914 as a lieutenant in the Cameronians (Scottish Rifles); his younger brother and his parents' only other child, a subaltern in the Royal Scots, had been killed twelve days before.

John Murray Archive, MS. 40556

The Gaelic World
12

12.1 Medical manuscript in need of health cure

THE ADVOCATES' LIBRARY acquired its first Gaelic manuscript in 1698, and more were bought in 1736 from the bookseller Robert Freebairn. Thereafter there were only a few further donations until the Highland Society of London's large collection, deposited with the Highland Society of Scotland in 1803, was transferred by that body (by then called the Highland and Agricultural Society of Scotland) to the Advocates' Library in 1850. The manuscript shown here, one of those purchased from Freebairn, is a girdle book, known as 'Neil MacBeath's Psalter' – which gives a rather misleading idea of its specific purpose, and conceals the fact that two different men of that name were responsible for its compilation. It is in fact a doctor's companion, containing religious and medical texts in both Gaelic and Latin. Small in size, and designed to be attached to a belt (hence its name), it would have been closed by wrapping the thong round the button on the front. This 'button' happens to be a sixteenth-century German jetton, a counter or token, with holes punched in it. The fifteenth- and sixteenth-century manuscript, now 'distressed' and looking much the worse for wear, might well benefit from one of the medical charms it contains. The MacBeaths, or Beatons, were members of a family of hereditary physicians.

Adv. MS. 72.1.4

12.2 Back-to-back worship

The small, planned town of Inveraray, at the head of Loch Fyne, was the conceit of the third Duke of Argyll. He enlisted William Adam as his architect and Adam and his sons also supervised the construction of the 'Gothick' toy-fort of Inveraray Castle, designed by Roger Morris. The town lay on a cultural 'fault-line', between a progressive Lowland Scotland that looked south to Hanoverian England, and a more traditional West Highland, Gaelic-speaking world. John Adam, William's eldest son, therefore designed a circular church to accommodate two congregations, one English-speaking, one Gaelic. The plan and section of this dual-natured building are shown here; the church is bisected by a dividing wall, with two back-to-back pulpits reached by a central, circular stair. The galleries have arcades carried on Roman Doric columns supported on free-standing piers, and a clerestory lights the whole interior. Sadly, John Adam's intriguing design was not executed, and it was left to Robert Mylne at the end of the eighteenth century to provide the town with a less exciting dual-function, back-to-back, Lowland-Highland church on a rectangular plan. The principal source for the building history of Inveraray town and castle is the papers of Andrew Fletcher, Lord Milton, a judge and politician, and a member of the Fletcher of Saltoun family, who acted as Argyll's agent in Scotland.

Saltoun Papers, MS. 17879 (2)

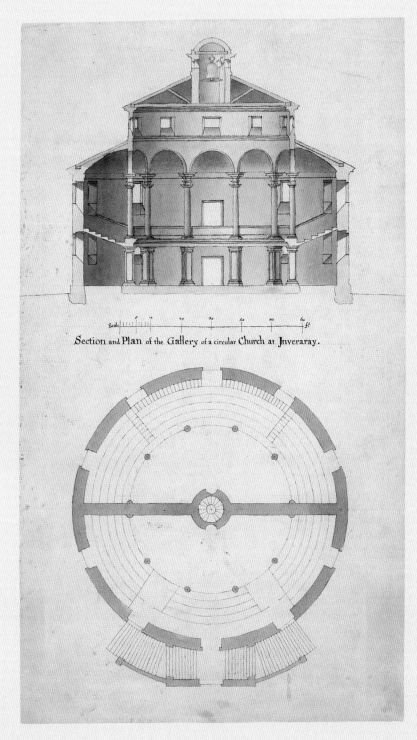

Section and Plan of the Gallery of a circular Church at Inveraray.

12.3 Napoleon's Ossian

THIS ELEGANT BINDING from Napoleon's library at Fontainebleau, with his imperial arms incorporating traditional symbols of the French monarchy he had usurped, ornaments a copy of the poems of Ossian. Napoleon was a great admirer of the work of this legendary Gaelic poet, which was largely, in fact, the creation of James Macpherson. Lord Rosebery wrote of Napoleon communing with the bard 'as with an old friend', and a copy accompanied him even to the field of Waterloo, as part of his travelling library of some 800 volumes. This copy is a two-volume French translation of 1798-99 which bears upon its title-pages the date '*An VII*' of the Revolutionary calendar, and the publisher's address in 'Palais-Égalité', better known before and since as Palais-Royal. Whether as a result of his enthusiasm for Ossian or for some other reason, Napoleon seems to have been interested in 'primitive' Highland culture. The Library also has a book

(L.C. 256), bound in identical style but stamped 'Malmaison', which is a French translation of Samuel Johnson's *Journey to the Western Islands of Scotland*, published in Paris in 1805 (Year XII). The emperor's admiration for Scotland and the Scots may have taken a rather different turn when his army in Portugal and Spain came up against Scottish troops (as it frequently did) or when at Waterloo he marvelled at the intrepidity of the Scots Greys in their famous charge against his advancing infantry. The Library has major holdings in the field of Ossianic material, notably the collection of J. Norman Methven, presented in 1941, which runs from the first edition of James Macpherson's first work, *Fragments of Ancient Poetry* (1760) to many subsequent translations of this, and of *Fingal* and *Temora*, in fine European editions reflecting the phenomenal popularity of the controversial verse.
Bdg. s. 792

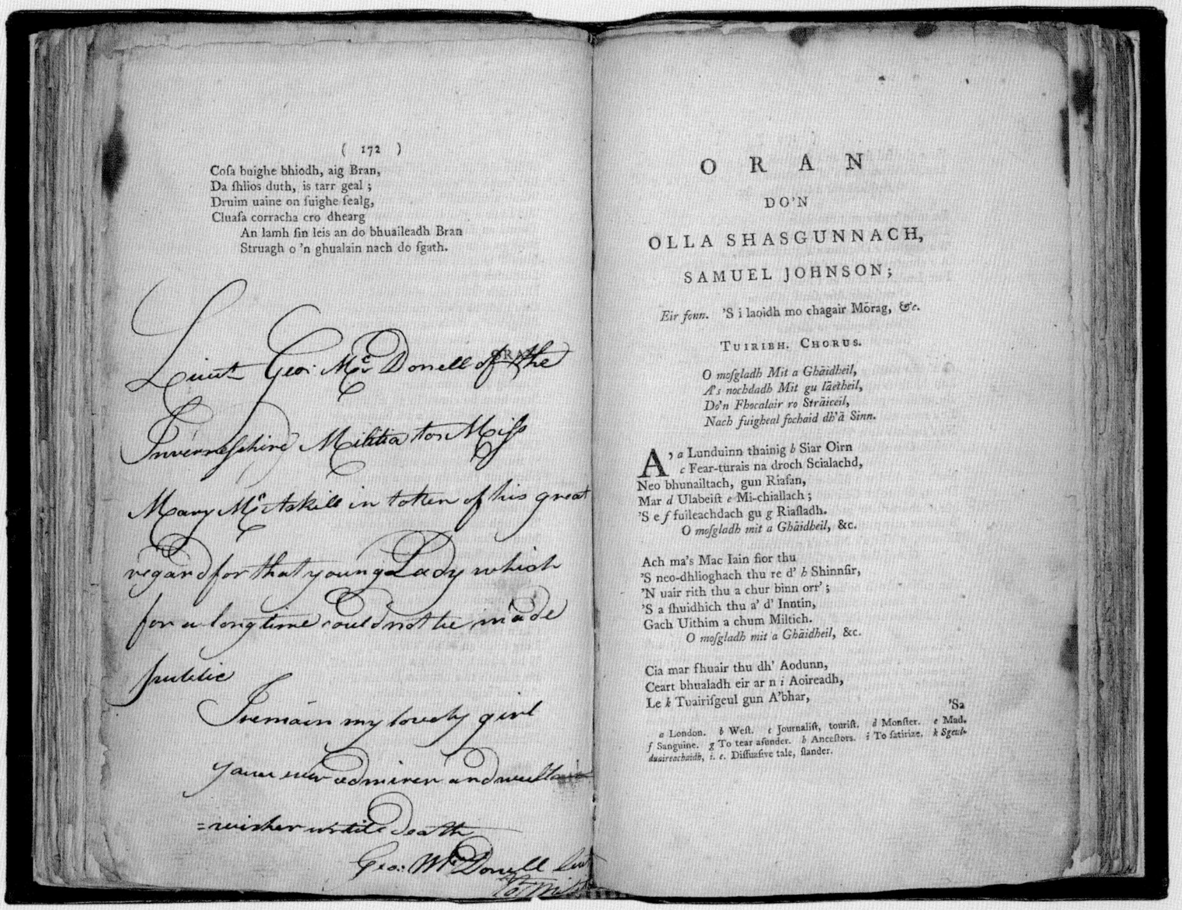

12.4 **The way to a girl's heart**

IT CANNOT BE A common experience for a woman to be wooed with a Gaelic poem attacking Dr Samuel Johnson as a 'mad, monster, journalist-tourist'. But this is precisely the suit that Miss Mary McAskill received from her beau, Lieutenant George McDonell of the Invernessshire Militia, when quartered in Edinburgh in 1805. On the page of a collection of Gaelic verse and songs shown here, the love-sick soldier states that he gives the book 'in token of his great regard for that young Lady which for a long time could not be made public. I remain my lovely girl your new admirer and well-wisher until death…' Lieutenant McDonell had evidently chosen to give his beloved a book that he already owned and which had been well-thumbed. He had also been practising his statement of devotion, for there are two 'trial' inscriptions elsewhere in the volume. Johnson's famous journey to the Hebrides with James Boswell in 1773 resulted in one of the classic travel accounts in English literature, to be followed by Boswell's equally celebrated account published just after Johnson's death. Johnson had been remarkably sympathetic in many of his attitudes, but some of his observations and opinions made his book anathema to Highlanders, hence this vituperative poem about 'MacIain' (Johnson) and his 'slanders'.

Sean dàin agus órain Ghaidhealach (Perth, 1786)

Mat. 178

12.5 Highland heritage

THE HIGHLAND SOCIETY of London was established in 1778 by Highland gentlemen in the capital, where Scots formed a notable and 'upwardly-mobile', if not always popular, community. Its objective was the 'improvement' – a characteristic eighteenth-century idea – of the Highlands and their people, and its interests were the preservation of the traditions, martial spirit, language, dress, music and antiquities of 'the ancient Caledonians'. The original aims included that of 'rescuing from Oblivion the valuable remains of Celtic Literature' and the society amassed large collections of Gaelic manuscripts, which came to the Advocates' Library in 1850 (cf. 12.1). The society, which was later to compile a valuable archive of specimens of tartan, was instrumental in securing the repeal, in 1782, of the act that had proscribed the wearing of Highland dress and tartan

after the defeat of the Jacobite rising of 1745-46. By this time the British government had seen the sense of establishing new Highland regiments and the army already wore the kilt, despite its civilian proscription. Proud of what these regiments achieved, the society struck commemorative medals for Highland troops after the battle of Alexandria in 1801 (cf.4.12); these were designed by the American neoclassical painter Benjamin West, president of the Royal Academy. West also designed this splendid diploma, heavy with Ossianic imagery and ornamented with muscular 'noble savages', who possess also a Roman dignity. Society branches abroad were established in British colonies, such as the Cape of Good Hope, and in theatres of war, for instance (as here) among British army officers in the Iberian peninsula.

Acc. 12518

JAMES LOGAN was an Aberdonian who found himself unable to pursue his intended legal career, due to being hit on the head by a hammer thrown during Highland games – possibly the ultimate injury for a true Gael to sustain, if the missile were not a (full) bottle of whisky. Instead he became the leading exponent of Gaelic history, customs, traditions and what he called 'national peculiarities' and was briefly secretary of the Highland Society of London. *The Scottish Gaël*; published in 1831 by the London Scottish house of Smith, Elder & Co., remains a seminal work of Scottish cultural history and anthropology. It was the result of Logan's observations made in many walking tours through the Highlands. This attractive plate is the frontispiece of the second volume: it is after a drawing by Logan himself, of a piper wearing the tartan of the 42nd Regiment – that is the Black Watch, or government tartan, which formed the uniform of the Royal Highland Regiment. This unit, which

had greatly distinguished itself in the French wars, had seen its uniform become a fashion item in which the ladies of Edinburgh had decked themselves in wartime, as Jessy Harden (cf. 8.8) testifies. Tartan; pipes; traditional weapons of broadsword and dirk; feather bonnet; elaborate sporran of varied regimental pattern: all these, decking the brawny Highland form, combined to make a powerfully martial and virile image before which half the world swooned and the other (male) half shrank. Here the figure is probably civilian, as the pipe banner bearing the royal arms would surely be unusual and unlikely to meet Lord Lyon's approval, and the 'uniform' is a stagey pastiche. But the overall effect of the piper playing before a castle that is Edinburgh, but in the setting of Stirling, captures the essence of romantic Scotland.

JAMES LOGAN, *The Scottish Gaël; or, Celtic Manners, as Preserved among the Highlanders*, 2 vols (London, 1831)

L.C. 1151

'TEUCHTER' IS A disparaging and even slightly contemptuous name for Gaelic-speaking Highlanders and Islanders, who appeared to Lowland and urban eyes as, by turns, uncouth, backward and idle. This has long been dismissed as patronising nonsense with little or no basis in actual fact, past or present. But even if this were not the case, the remarkably-titled *TCS sa 2LG*, a text-messaging

guide launched in 2003 for the use of tech-savvy young people north of the Highland line, finally lays the myth to rest. It is tempting to see the boxing-gloved, jack-in-the-box fist as symbolic of a new generation striking back against the prejudices of the past.

[MARLENE GILLES] *TCS sa 2LG*

PB5. 208. 188/6

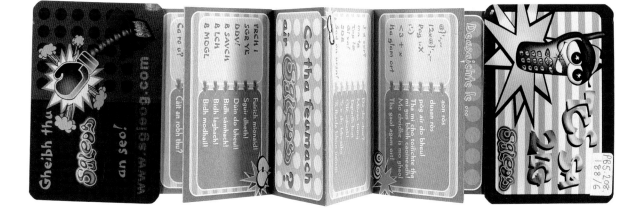

Discoveries of Scotland 13

13.1 Disaster at Ossian's Hall

The Tour of Doctor Prosody, in Search of the Antique and Picturesque through Scotland… (1821) is a superb satire on the vogue for Scottish travel (cf. 11.4). William Combe caught the fashion beautifully and mocked it gently, but to brilliant effect. The English clergyman of antiquarian turn of mind does all the things visitors of his kind most enjoyed: hobnobbing with the *literati* of Edinburgh, visiting Highland chiefs in their castles, and seeing the great natural and historic sites, attended the while by strong-willed Highland servants. Combe's clever rhyming couplets are perfectly matched by the amusing aquatint plates. Here Prosody and his friend Dr Fac-

tobend, accompanied by Archie the servant in his trews and Highland bonnet, and by the tourists' dog, are seen at Ossian's Hall at the Hermitage overlooking the falls of the River Braan, near Dunkeld in Perthshire. The Duke of Atholl's tourist-trap 'visitor attraction' (as it might now be called) was fitted with mirror glass, creating a disorientating optical allusion that water was cascading everywhere. Images are multiplied and the travelling dog, seeing himself over and over, runs amuck and, in the ensuing chaos, Dr Factobend breaks the mirrors – and Dr Prosody's concentration on drawing the view. Hall. 151.d

13.2 Please do write in this book

SOMETIMES LIBRARIES should be pleased that their books have been written in or otherwise defaced. Allan Ramsay's note about his use of the Bannatyne Manuscript (cf. 10.1) helps illustrate the succession of influences and inheritors of tradition in literary history. The copy of George Buchanan's *Rerum Scoticarum Historia* (1582) which was Montaigne's, and which bears his signature upon the title-page, is further enhanced by the comment of a less admiring though anonymous reader who scored out the author's name and substituted the epithet 'haeretico maledicto' (RB. m. 16). James Boswell borrowed from the Advocates' Library (as he was entitled to do) a copy of Martin Martin's book on the Western Isles and took it with him when he made his famous journey with Samuel Johnson in 1773. He returned it safely the next year, having written a note on the verso of the title-page recording the book's adventure and commenting on Martin's deficiencies, while at the same time offering somewhat patronising praise of his poor efforts: 'His Book is a very imperfect performance; & he is erroneous as to many particulars… I cannot but have a kindness for him notwithstanding his defects.' Many, when reading this last sentence, might have Bozzy himself in mind. A copy of Martin's work had come into the hands of the youthful Johnson, who had been fascinated by this account, by a native of Skye, of a society so different from his own. This early, vicarious encounter with the Western Isles was the ultimate inspiration for what would be perhaps the single most important exploration of those regions ever to take place.

MARTIN MARTIN, *A Description of the Western Islands of Scotland* (London, 1703)
H. 32. a. 31

13.3 Caledonia imagined

Dr Johnson at least conquered his prejudices and visited Scotland. Other Englishmen, such as Dr William Stukeley, wrote of the country and its antiquities without benefit of seeing for himself. Stukeley was a physician turned clergyman. He was also a pioneer field archaeologist, whose important work was compromised by a highly eccentric temperament and an obsession with druidic theories. He became interested in a mysterious structure known as 'Arthur's O'on' (i.e. oven) which stood north of the Antonine Wall near Falkirk. Several contemporary antiquaries also showed interested in this building, which was considered to be a Roman temple or shrine of a highly unusual type – but which may, in fact, have been a medieval pottery kiln. Having written about it in a pamphlet of 1720, Stukeley returned to the subject of Arthur's O'on (which in the meantime had

been destroyed by an ignorant and unscrupulous landowner in 1743, much to the outrage of the British antiquarian community) in the context of his wider researches into the career of the Romano-British usurper Carausius, who declared himself emperor of Britain. In his learned but eccentric treatise, Stukeley included two drawings of Arthur's O'on in aggressively 'Scottish' settings, with kilted men riding beside it, or on guard with the Highland hills behind, and with giant thistles ornamenting the foreground. Stukeley's concern for a building he had never seen, in a country he had never visited, illustrates an aspect of Scottish discovery more unusual than most.

WILLIAM STUKELEY, *The Medallic History of Marcvs Avrelivs Valerivs Caravsivs, Emperor in Brittain* (London, 1757-59)
E.66.c.2

13.4 'Mine own romantic town'

IT IS IMPOSSIBLE to over-estimate the importance of Walter Scott's role in popularising the history, traditions (whether invented by him or otherwise) and legends, scenery, and indeed everything else connected with Scotland. In *The Lay of the Last Minstrel* (1805) he extolled a man's passion for his own country: 'Breathes there the man, with soul so dead, /Who never to himself hath said, /This is my own, my native land!' In *Marmion* (1808), he focused more narrowly upon the Border landscape and on his native city, his description inspiring countless visitors to see Auld Reekie. The Waverley novels, the finest of which have Scottish topographical and historical settings

(these being what Scott knew best and could do best, when 'his foot was upon his native heath') brought even more travellers north to a country and a romantic world that Scott had opened to them. The evocation of Edinburgh on the eve of Flodden, in Canto IV of *Marmion*, remains one of the best-known such descriptions in literature. The autograph manuscript was bequeathed to the Advocates' Library in 1898. In this image the manuscript rests on Scott's writing-box, also in the Library, which bears an inscription by John Ballantyne recording the fact that the poem, and other earlier work, had been written upon it.

Adv. MS. 19.1.16

13.5 Europeans take a peep

THIS PEEPSHOW of Edinburgh, of about 1830, is characteristic of the rage for Scotland and all things Scottish that gripped Europe as a direct result of Scott's wildly popular narrative poems, and his all-conquering success as a writer of prose fiction. Scott had familiarised all Europe with the buildings of Edinburgh, and of Scotland as a whole, with the history they had witnessed and the landscape in which they stood. Thus, for example, François Alexandre Pernot and Amédée Pichot's *Vues Pittoresques de l'Écosse* (Paris and Brussels, 1826 and 1827) represented a visual and verbal tour of Scott's Scotland. And at the very outset of his *Skottska Vuer* (Stockholm 1831), Carl Samuel Graffman made it clear that his interpretation of what constituted Scottish history and landscape (to which the accompanying lithographs by C.-J. Billmark

paid visual tribute) was indebted first to Macpherson, with his Ossian poems, and then to Scott, with his literary evocation of the country. The title-page of *Skottska Vuer* carries a very similar view of Edinburgh Castle from the Grassmarket to that adorning this German peepshow. The game expands, concertina-wise, so that the view at the back of the resulting 'box' is the same as that at the front. Intervening coloured sheets act like flats in a theatre, giving a credible idea of perspective to the scene. Life and movement abound. The three apertures give the spectator additional townscape scenes, interior views and romantic ruin-prospects of differing character.

Le Château d'Edinbourg. Das Schloss zu Edinburg. The Castle of Edinburgh.

FB.s.378

from Glasgow to Dumbarton; brought by road to Balloch, jolting in 'moving penitentiaries'; embarked for the 20-mile loch voyage; offered a choice of refreshment and activity on the loch-side at Rowardennan, whence Ben Lomond might be attempted; embarked in the *Marian* again; besieged by local urchins offering to help with baggage and demanding 'bawbees' (gratuities), subject of another very good illustration; transported ('hoiked') back from Balloch to Dumbarton in more 'ricketty, disjointing, cramping machines'; stowed again in a boat and returned up the Clyde to Glasgow. Egerton shows himself, dressed as the compete traveller, setting out for his Scottish tour in a wry plate at the opening of his book.

M[ICHAEL] E[GERTON], *Airy Nothings; or, Scraps and Naughts, and Odd-Cum-Shorts; in a Circumbendibus Hop, Step and Jump, by Olio Rigmaroll* (London, 1825)

FB. m. 150

13.6 'A local habitation and a name'

Airy Nothings is a delightful travel book, with charming plates and a very odd text. 'Olio Rigmaroll' describes a trip on Loch Lomond in the *Marian* steamboat. His own illustrations add much attractive detail and local colour, from the piper who plays to the tourists on board, to the sightseers' use of telescopes to spy out the beauty-spots on the bonnie banks. This was 'package tourism' at its inception. The author describes how passengers for the excursion were shipped

13.7 The signal for the boat

IN COMMENTING ON this plate of a Highland couple beside their 'boat fire' while waiting for transport across a loch, James Logan writes interestingly of the economic benefits of tourism in the Highlands, but of progress also having its detrimental effects. Before the age of organised steamboat travel, on what were effectively package tours from Glasgow to Staffa, Iona, the Caledonian Canal, and other destinations, inde-

pendent travellers had been obliged to summon local boatmen much as the native inhabitants are shown doing here. In these ways, Logan says, 'a considerable amount of money was left among the Highlanders, while the intercourse was in other respects beneficial. It is quite otherwise now…that steam boats ply all around'. Travellers 'pass through the country, without perhaps leaving a shilling behind. The poor Highlanders feel the loss of this source, whence a seasonable accession to their scanty means was often obtained'. This view of what Logan terms a 'Celtic Trajectus' serves to remind us that the inhabitants, too, were travellers in their own land, and that they made discoveries within a more limited topographical ambit.

R. R. MCIAN & JAMES LOGAN, *Picturesque Gatherings of the Scottish Highlanders at Home, on the Heath, the River, and the Loch: a Series of Highly Interesting Plates, Representing Picturesque Groups Engaged in their Social Employment, their Sports, and Pastimes* (London, 1848)

FB.l.220

13.8 **Queen of hearts**

THE LIFE AND DEATH of the tragic Mary, Queen of Scots, inspired much contemporary writing of an almost hagiographic character, in Catholic Europe as well as in recusant Britain. This was, of course, balanced by the vituperative attacks of Protestant theologians such as John Knox and his successors. Her memory lived on as a roseate romance, given added poignancy first by the execution of her grandson Charles, 'king and martyr', in 1649, and then by the lost cause of the exiled Stuart dynasty in the abortive Jacobite risings of the '15 and the '45. A high point in romantic devotion was the ball given in the Tuileries by Charles X of France in 1829, the year before his abdication after the July Revolution and his forced return to Scotland, where he had previously been in exile at Holyroodhouse in the 1790s. The ball was a magnificent occasion at which Mary was portrayed by the Duchesse de Berry, the king's daughter-in-law, wearing a costume based on a portrait of the queen by François Clouet. The British ambassador to Paris, Lord Stuart de Rothesay (whose papers are in the Library) and his wife (who took part as Mary of Guise) and daughter (as a rather fetching page to the character her mother played) were present among a great assemblage of notables dressed in splendid sixteenth-century costume. This superb book of lithographs records an event that seems in retrospect another anthem for a doomed regime.

EUGÈNE LOUIS LAMI, *Quadrille de Marie Stuart. 11 mars 1829* (Paris, 1829) FB.l.137

13.9 *La fièvre écossaise*

WALTER SCOTT, and the rage for Scotland that he and his works engendered, rendered everything 'Scotch' fashionable and fun. A ball and masquerade at the court of the king of Bavaria in Munich in 1835 make the point. The occasion was divided into two parts, both recorded in series of lithographed plates after watercolours by Ignaz Kürzinger, which were in turn based on sketches by Ernst Fries and Franz Xaver Nachtmann. First, there was a parade of characters in costume representing the countries of the world. The Comtesse de Tauffkirchen and the Baron de Möller-Lilienstern appeared kitted out in what Central Europeans thought was Scottish dress. Naturally there is tartan a-plenty; but there any attempt at verisimilitude peters out. The brevity of the baron's kilt, what looks like a War Office

broad-arrow on his sporran, and the oddity of the feather bonnets worn by the couple, render the ensembles ludicrous. The second part of the festivity was even more remarkable from the Scottish viewpoint. It took the form of a series of tableaux based upon Scott's novel *Quentin Durward* (1823), the book that really established his reputation in Europe. Only a dozen years later the *jeunesse dorée* of Bavaria were dressing up as no fewer than 27 characters from the book. The Prince de Salm Reiferscheid appeared as Lord Crawford, captain of the Scottish Guard of the king of France, and the Comte d'Arco Zinneberg as an archer of the Guard.

Quadrilles Parées Costumées Exécutées à la Cour de Sa Majesté le Roi de Bavière le 3 Fevrier 1835 (Munich [1835])

FB. l. 239

13.10 'Here is hubby in his tartan, I hope you think he is a smartun'

THE LIBRARY HAS long collected records of travellers to Scotland. The nineteenth century saw a great increase in visitor numbers and in the production of travel journals. One of the most appealing diaries is that of a recently-married couple from Ireland who visited Scotland in the late summer and autumn of 1849. We know them only as Nan (who kept the journal) and Fred. But we also know exactly what they did, and how much it all cost: the volume includes accounts detailing such matters as charges for transport, accommodation and provisions; entry to Edinburgh Castle, Holyroodhouse and various country houses and gardens; repairs to boots; sixpence paid to the guide at

Rosslyn Chapel; and the cost of buying articles of 'Scotch' clothing and for making up a tartan dress for Nan and a plaid for Fred. Freshwater pearls and cairngorms (yellow quartz) were set for them by an Edinburgh jeweller. The holiday-makers enjoyed themselves on loch and hill, doing what they saw as typical Highland things: drinking a little whisky, paddling in clear spring water, climbing mountains in the mist, walking through 'the pith and marrow of Highland scenery'. These activities were recorded in charmingly naive drawings, with speech-bubble comments, pasted into the diary.

Acc. 12615

13.11 Rambles with pen and palette

SEVERAL OF THE BEST accounts of nineteenth-century Scotland, both verbal and visual, were by French visitors. They seemed to have a knack of expressing the essence of what it was about Scotland that so appealed to the romantic sensibilities of Europe as a whole between about 1820 and 1860. Charles Nodier, with *Promenade de Dieppe aux Montagnes d'Écosse* (1821) and Amédée Pichot, with *Historical and Literary Tour of a Foreigner* (1825), the latter of whom had timed his visit to coincide with that of George IV to Edinburgh in 1822, stand at the forefront of this procession of Gallic admirers. The artists quickly followed. One of the most striking productions is Michel

Bouquet's *Scotland* and its lithographed title-page is particularly effective, with the lettering standing like some surreal prehistoric stone circle rising from the waters of Loch Ness below Urquhart Castle. The plates in Bouquet's collection, which result from visits he made with his fellow artist Sulpice-Guillaume Chevalier, known as Gavarni, are striking in their portrayal of the grandeur and wildness of scenery, and in their use of dramatic lighting effects.

MICHEL BOUQUET, *Scotland. The Tourist's Rambles in the Highlands* (Paris [c.1850])

FB. el. 103

SCOTLAND

THE TOURIST'S RAMBLES
IN THE HIGHLANDS

BY MICHEL BOUQUET

Urquhart Castle
Loch Ness

13.12 **A genteel occupation**

THE WORLD OF THE Victorian house-party in a Highland shooting-lodge is captured perfectly in the drawings and sketchbooks in the Ellice of Invergarry Papers. Edward Ellice (d. 1863) and his son Edward (d. 1880) were prominent Liberal members of Parliament. They were rich and well-connected landowners in Scotland, Canada, the US and the West Indies; most of the Victorian political and social establishment seems, at one time or another, to have made its way north to stay with the Ellices at their shooting lodge at Glenquoich. How visitors spent their time is recorded in many competent drawings and watercolours, of which this is a typical example. Outdoors the guests stalk, shoot, fish, walk, climb hills in crinolines, sail, and see how crofters live in humble cottages. Indoors they read, write, talk, paint, smoke, eat heartily and, quite possibly (though we do not actually see this), conduct affairs along draughty bedroom corridors. In an age of the talented amateur, art was an important part of the lives of ladies and gentlemen staying in such a place in such company, where a real artist, Landseer, was also an occasional houseguest: drawings by him form part of the Ellice Papers. Lady Grey is shown 'in her element', sketching the scene from her window. Amusing notices are pinned up: instructions to revive her, if found insensible, with hot water and mustard baths, or to bring tots of brandy in the night.

MS. 15174, no. 32

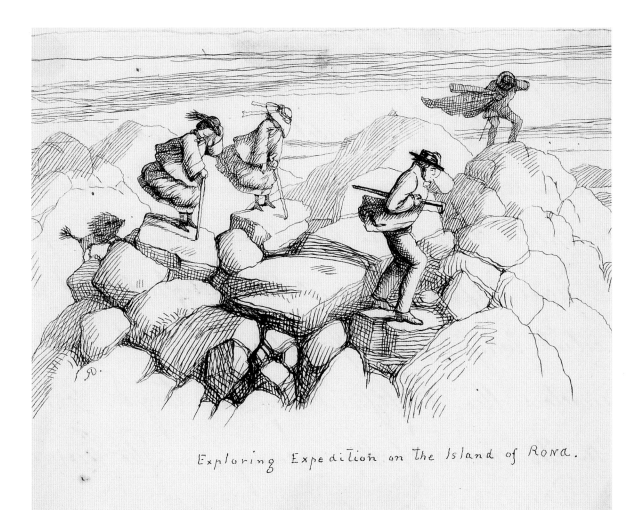

Exploring Expedition on the Island of Rona.

13.13 A bracing walk

IN 1859 RICHARD ('DICKIE') DOYLE, illustrator and celebrated *Punch* cartoonist, accompanied the Ellice family
and friends on a short autumn voyage in the yacht *Ladye*
from Loch Hourn to Lewis and Skye. His 'log' of the sail
is made all the more delightful by its pen and ink illustrations, showing what the passengers got up to on board
and at the various places where landfall was made. The
log shares a portfolio with a series of sketches made by
Doyle in 1855, when he sailed in the other Ellice boat,
the *Lotus*, to Skye and Rona. The visual record of this trip
has no accompanying narrative. Here a 'landing party'
is buffeted by wind on the hills of the island; Scotland,
though popular as a tourist destination, could sometimes
demand a great deal of her would-be admirers.

Ms. 15150

13.14
The Russians are coming

'Discovery' of a somewhat different
kind lay behind the making of the Russian map shown here. The icy winds of the
Cold War blow across Scotland in a series
of maps, based on Ordnance Survey
originals and produced with a military
purpose lest that war ever turn hot. The
creation of employment for an army of
linguists, cartographers, engravers and
printers may also have been in the mind
of the authorities who ordered the preparation of these maps, even into the 1980s.
The detailed work expended on them is
remarkable. On large-scale maps, the
depth of rivers and the width of bridges
is given, along with statistics and meas-
urements that might have been useful if
invasion were launched. Even relatively
small-scale maps must have involved
a great effort in transliteration, with
familiar names appearing in Cyrillic
characters. This sectional map of the
western half of the capital takes in areas
of widely differing character, with the
harbour of Granton, the suburbs of
Trinity, Davidson's Mains, Corstorphine,
Saughtonhall, Stenhouse and Murray-
field, the inner districts of Inverleith and
Comely Bank, and the geometrical grid-
patterns of the New Town and West End
prominent, recognisable and readable
despite the 'camouflage'. Edinburgh has
traditionally been said to be 'east-windy
and west-endy', a remark that captures
the essence of its weather and its once-
prevailing social attitudes. At the bottom
right is the iconic, very 'Edinburgh',
district of Morningside, a byword for
gentility and correct behaviour where,
in the 1970s, the density of fur-coat
wearers per head of population might
have made Russian soldiers with snow
on their boots or hatchet-faced KGB
agents feel at home. But Russian political
ideas might have found a more sympathetic hearing in Gorgie or Pilton.

Map. 1.88.31

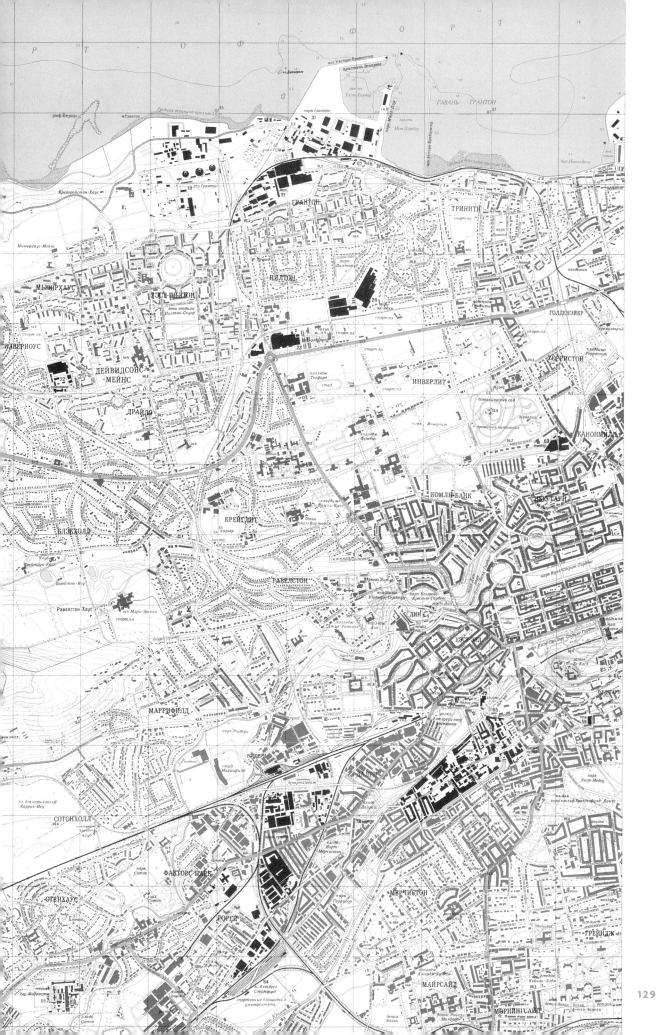

ФОРТ

ГАВАНЬ ГРАНТОН

КРЕЙГРОЙСТОН-ХАУС

ГРАНТОН

ТРИНИТИ

ГОЛДЕНЭЙКР

МЬЮРХАУС-МЕЙНС

НИЛТОН

МЬЮРХАУС

УЭСТ-ПИЛТОН

УОРРИСТОН

ИНВЕРНОУС

ИНВЕРЛИТ

КАНОНМИЛЛ

ДЕЙВИДСОНС-МЕЙНС

ДРАЙЛО

 КОМЛИ-БАНК

НЬЮ-ТАУН

БЛЭКХОЛЛ

КРЕЙГЛИТ

РАВЕЛСТОН

ДИН

Равелстон-Хаус

УЭСТ-ЭНД

ОЛД-ТАУН

МАРРИФИЛД

ДАЛРИ

МЕРЧИСТОН

СОТОНХОЛЛ

ФАКТОРС-ПАРК

СТЕНХАУС

ГРЕЙНДЖ

ГОРГИ

МАЙРСАЙД

МОРНИНГСАЙД

129

Diversities and Diversions of Life

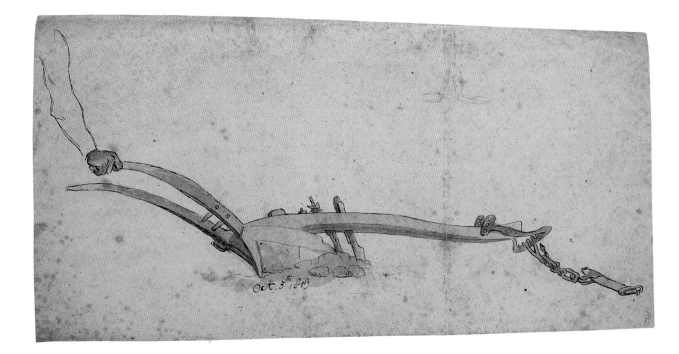

14.1 **The heaven-taught ploughman's plough**

IN ROBERT BURNS'S DAY, Scotland was overwhelmingly an agricultural society: the poet himself was a farmer and turned this to his advantage, recognising the surprise of the Edinburgh *literati* that a man from what they saw as a humble station in life should be capable of writing verse of such power and sensibility, or letters of such Augustan elegance and style. Reviewing the Kilmarnock volume of poems in *The Lounger* in December 1786, Henry Mackenzie praised 'this Heaven-taught ploughman', and so ensured Burns's social and literary success in Edinburgh that winter. The half-real, half-mythical appeal of the 'ploughman poet' never left Burns. In 1808 Robert Hartley Cromek

published his *Reliques of Robert Burns*. A grangerised (i.e. with additional material bound in post-publication) copy in the Library includes some drawings of Burns memorabilia and scenes connected with the poet. These were by Thomas Stothard, perhaps the most distinguished book-illustrator of the day, for Cromek's projected edition of the poet's works. This one shows the actual plough with which the poet turned up the mouse and the daisy. For Burns, the plough was a symbol both of honest toil and of the disruptive hand of man on nature. The hand steadying the implement is that of the poet's brother, Gilbert. MS. 1655, f. 102

14.2 **The silver darlings**

FISHING WAS THE other staple of pre-industrial
Scotland. Many crofters, driven from the land in the
Highland clearances, were forced to seek a living
from the unforgiving sea. In times of plenty it offered
a profitable means of subsistence, but always with
the threat of loss of boats and men. As Scott put it
memorably in *The Antiquary* (1816), 'it's no fish ye're
buying – it's men's lives'. The herring were known as
'the silver darlings', and that is the title of Neil Gunn's
novel of 1941 (Gunn's papers are in the Library). In
1867 John Francis Campbell had made this watercolour sketch of fishermen bringing in their catch off
North Berwick, a harbour-town on the East Lothian

coast which would become a prosperous holiday
resort serving Edinburgh, a status it still maintains
when so much of the rest of the Scottish seaside has
died. Campbell of Islay, whose extensive papers
came to the Advocates' Library by bequest in 1885,
belonged to a Highland gentry family. A public servant and courtier, he was and also a major figure in
the collection and publication of Gaelic folk-lore.
Passionately interested in ethnography and all manner of scientific enquiry, he travelled very widely
and very far from Scotland. Illustration was vital to
all his studies, and he was an accomplished artist.
Adv. MS. 50.4.2, f. 187

14.3 Black gold

DEEP COAL-MINING was another great Scottish industry which is now almost a memory. The remarkable Hiram Sturdy, of Newarthill, Lanarkshire (cf. 4.17), left a series of evocative drawings and watercolours illustrating every aspect of the mining life, and of the tight-knit communities that were the pit-villages before and after the First World War. Here he shows a group of miners making its way along partly-flooded workings. The commentary nicely catches the fear and the heroism, but also the good-humour and the comradeship, that were a frequent part of the miner's life. Sturdy drew various scenes of mining disaster or near-disaster: floods, roof-falls, gas escapes, explosions, accidents and injury due to machinery malfunction, mishandling or human carelessness. But he also recorded the brighter aspects of the pit-village life in communal activity or in individual domestic settings.

Dep. 279/ 32

14.4 The best days of their lives

THE SCOTS USED TO be justly proud of an educational system which penetrated even to the poorest and most remote corners of the land. This plate, by Robert McIan, shows boys in Lochaber trudging willingly – if chillily – through snow to school. They carry with them their school books held in straps: we can see that the central child carries a thick Bible and a Latin grammar among other volumes. All the boys bear peats for the school fire. They are led by the so-called Boy of the Horn, a poor barefoot child who assumed this duty for one penny per quarter paid by his fellow schoolboys; his duty appears to have been to 'encourage the others' on their harsh walk to school through wind and weather. The illustration comes from a fine volume of plates with a commentary by James Logan (cf. 2.4). Here Logan comments on the health and hardiness of these 'ragged-looking, bare-legged urchins', whom he reckoned to be fitter than children 'whose parents wrap them in more comfortable-looking garments'. Logan goes on to observe that the children are 'of sharp intellect; and there are few boys in the Highlands of twelve or fourteen years of age who cannot read and write'. As to girls, Logan is completely silent.

R. R. MCIAN & JAMES LOGAN, *Picturesque Gatherings of the Scottish Highlanders at Home, on the Heath, the River, and the Loch: a Series of Highly Interesting Plates, Representing Picturesque Groups Engaged in their Social Employment, their Sports, and Pastimes* (London, 1848)

FB.l.220

Fish Balls.

Take the remains of any kind of white fish (which first you must catch) Chop it very fine, and mix with an equal quantity of mashed Potatoes, salt, pepper and butter. Mix all these together, & make them into small round cakes. Egg them, bread them, Crumb them, and fry them in hot Lard.
The parties here delineated
will do the catching part in
the most first rate Style.
Need I mention. Lady Harriett S! Clair
& Ms E. Ellice.

Janie. E.

14.5 Bouncing billys, friar's chicken and fish balls

THIS CHARMING AND delightful recipe book with a difference is the work of Katharine Jane Ellice, a member of the prominent and influential Invergarry family. The Ellice Papers have long been in the Library but the present book had strayed from this archive and was bought in 2003. It captures beautifully and memorably the world of Victorian fishing- and shooting-parties in Highland lodges, all fuelled by gargantuan meals. The volume complements other fine illustrated diaries, visitors' books, etc.,

in the Ellice Papers, some by this same young woman, whose work as a whole forms an excellent record of the activities of her friends and contemporaries among the Victorian gentry at leisure or sport, and of their servants at work feeding and maintaining them. The whimsicality of 'Janie' Ellice's culinary vision is admirably illustrated in her recipe for 'Fish Balls', where salmon, freshly landed, play with jugglers' balls.

Acc. 12266

14.6 A Scottish Christmas in London

THE PAINTER David Roberts was miserably married, but had the great consolation of a much-loved only daughter. In due course Christine Roberts married Henry Bicknell, son of one of Roberts's (and Turner's) most significant patrons; and the ageing Roberts found great happiness in her expanding family. Roberts was genial and enjoyed the company of his own wide circle of friends in art and society. He maintained his Edinburgh connections: the Library (among a very large quantity of Roberts correspondence) holds two volume of his letters to David Ramsay Hay, the eminent interior decorator and colour theorist. In this letter of 1852, Roberts writes from London to describe the pleasure that Hay's Christmas presents of traditional Scottish 'black bun' and short-bread had given the Bicknell family in their house at Brixton. The black bun had provoked some real interest through its evident novelty at a Sassenach table. Its merits, and its differences from and similarities to plum pudding, had been debated, and the question had been raised as to whether people in Scotland lived on shortbread all the year round. Roberts's letter bears marks looking suspiciously like wine stains. It would have arrived in Edinburgh before Hogmanay, just in time to be caught up in Hay family New Year festivities; if perhaps a bottle had then been overturned, the evidence is preserved for all time.

MS. 3522, f. 158

14.8 'Wi' usquabea, we'll face the devil!'

WHEN BURNS mentioned whisky, it was very largely a drink of the lower classes, and so it remained until well into the nine-teenth century, though King George IV apparently enjoyed a dram or two during his visit to Edinburgh in 1822. But in later Victorian times whisky became the drink of choice of the upper classes, and of the British Empire as a whole. This whisky, almost wholly of the blended malt and grain variety, was produced in industrial quantities and shrewdly advertised and marketed. It was drunk in a way that the whisky connoisseur would never approve – on ice and with soda water – and sold for its suggestion of gentlemanliness and its putative associations with the club, and a regimental or aristocratic way of life. Dewar's, in particular, ran a series of clever advertisements in the press, and even in early film, featuring 'The Whisky of his Ancestors', based on a painting by Septimus Edwin Scott which was adapted and updated through the years. The owner of an ancestral pile, and current holder of a title, relaxes with his dram. The portraits on the walls, redolent of the historic past of family and nation and wearing the uniform of various wars and conflicts of history, come to life and reach from their frames for a sip from his glass or at least in the hope of catching the aroma of his drink.

The House of Dewar 1846–1946 (London, 1946) Q3.75.940

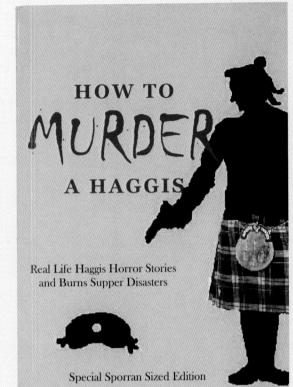

14.7 **Hagiography of the haggis**

EVERYONE KNOWS that haggis is Scotland's national dish. Not everyone likes it; not everyone knows, or wants to know, what is in it. Some even think it is a living creature (or was, before its cooking, ritual slaughter and disembowelling at a Burns supper) – but are not quite sure whether land-based, airborne, or even amphibian. All, however, appreciate that the haggis has a distinct identity and a redoubtable character. Burns, of course, stands at the head of the haggis-fancying fraternity. Without him the haggis would be far less honoured and far less universally enjoyed and appreciated, even if for some people that appreciation is a duty confined to the last week of January each year. The literature on the haggis continues to grow and two recent additions are shown. Clarissa Dickson Wright, professional 'Fat Lady' cook who trades happily on a rather haggis-shaped image herself, has written a jolly *Little History*, delightfully illustrated by Clare Hewitt. One picture illuminates a doubtless apocryphal episode when a haggis came to the aid of some fleeing Jacobites after Culloden. Rolling downhill from its overturned cooking-pot, the haggis impaled itself upon a Hanoverian bayonet and sprayed its boiling-hot contents over the redcoats, and the fugitives escaped. Deedee Cuddihy's offering is a sort of Burns supper companion, and is (on another level) an interesting example of desk-top publishing and computer-generated imagery: the 'Special Sporran Sized Edition' is in fact the book's only format.

CLARISSA DICKSON WRIGHT, *The Haggis. A Little History* (Belfast, 1996)

SP1.98.236

DEEDEE CUDDIHY, *How to Murder a Haggis* (Glasgow, 2007)

PB1.208.3412

14.9 **An illicit whisky still**

'IT IS A CURIOUS FACT, that the means of producing excitation, or a pleasing flow of animal spirits, is one of the earliest objects of human solicitude.' In this pompous way James Logan introduced his commentary on Robert McIan's dramatic image of two Highlanders watching the 'water of life' drip slowly but satisfyingly from the pipes of their illicit still during a Highland evening. Logan's text discusses the history of whisky distilling in Scotland and highlights an almost honourable tradition of avoiding the exciseman or 'gauger'. 'Caves in the mountains, coiries or hollows in the upland heaths, and recesses in the glens, are chosen for the purpose, and they are, from fear of detection, often abandoned after the first "brewst".'

R. R. McIAN & JAMES LOGAN, *Picturesque Gatherings of the Scottish Highlanders at Home, on the Heath, the River, and the Loch: a Series of Highly Interesting Plates, Representing Picturesque Groups Engaged in their Social Employment, their Sports, and Pastimes* (London, 1848)
FB.l.220

14.10 Votaries of Venus

EDINBURGH'S MOST celebrated madam of modern times, Dora Noyce, of elegant Danube Street in the New Town, used to say that the busiest time for her and her girls was the week of the General Assembly of the Church of Scotland. Believe that or not, it catches the air of sanctimony that had long surrounded the vice trade in the city. It was this stifling attitude that the young Robert Louis Stevenson ('Velvet Coat', as the whores called him), so detested in Edinburgh's hypocritical moral code. By contrast, it is interesting to discover that the copy of the little book shown here was purchased by Charles Kirkpatrick Sharpe in 1840 in the belief that one of the ladies of pleasure mentioned was a distant relative, and that the 'catalogue entry' on p. 35 for this 'Mrs, *alias* Lady, Agnew, Nether-bow', constituted a 'precious memorial of one of my female cousins'. She is listed as a 'drunken bundle of iniquity… about 50 years of age, lusty and tall… she would as willingly lie with a chimney-sweep as with a Lord. Her desires are so immoderate that she would think nothing of a company of Grenadiers at one time… she is an abandoned Piece.'

A 'catalogue' is what this slim volume is: the user might consult it on matters of age, size, complexion, hair-colour, teeth (very important), nature, personality, manners and intellectual attainments (yes, really), abilities, preferences, and even convenience of 'business address'.

Ranger's Impartial List of the Ladies of Pleasure in Edinburgh (Edinburgh, 1775)

Ry. II. g.23

14.11 *Memento mori*

FOOD, DRINK, SEX, death… There may be a logic to this arrangement of items. The splendid funeral invitation shown dates from 1738. David Simson, a lawyer or 'writer', was to be interred in Greyfriars kirkyard. Chief mourner was his 'brother-german' (that is his own brother, one 'closely akin'), a professor of medicine in the university of Edinburgh. The cortège would have been similar to that shown at the foot of the paper; some of the mourners are likely to have been professional 'weepers', supplied by the undertaker as part of his expensive service. There are clear stylistic parallels between the ornamental details of this invitation and the elaborate funerary monuments and tombstones which form such a striking and uniquely important feature of the city graveyard where the burial was to take place.

APS. 2. 205. 005

14.12
What you play in heaven

THERE ARE THOSE who would argue that eternity is a game of golf: pre-eminently *the* Scottish sport, almost all that is distinctive about the game originated, or was codified, in Scotland. The Honourable Company of Edinburgh Golfers (as it is now known, and which today is based at Muirfield, by Gullane, East Lothian) formulated the first rules of the game, had the first clubhouse, and was the first club to take responsibility for its own course. This diploma of 1787 is granted to William Robertson, Advocate, later a judge, son of the historian William Robertson. The vignette of a golfer wielding his club, before a profile of Edinburgh with its

castle seen from Leith Links, is engraved by David Lizars, *paterfamilias* of an Edinburgh dynasty long

prominent in the art (cf.1.5).
Robertson-Macdonald Papers, MS. 3988, no 7

14.13 Just jousting in the rain

OVER THREE WET DAYS in August 1839 the cream of society gathered at Eglinton Castle, Ayrshire, to witness and to take part in a re-creation of the rights of medieval chivalry. That the Eglinton Tournament took place at all was due in large measure to the still-radiant light of Sir Walter Scott's romantic dream of baronial derring-do. James Henry Nixon and John Richardson collaborated in the production of a luxurious illustrated record of an extravaganza the like of which had never been seen. It made such an impression that Benjamin Disraeli could still write of it in 1880 in his novel *Endymion*. The protagonists, in their armour, chain-mail, tabards and wimples, with their attendant esquires, pages, heralds and trumpeters, their retinues of archers, halberdiers

and duniewassles, the bevies of maidens in attendance upon the so-called 'Queen of Beauty', were prominent aristocratic or gentry figures. Prince Louis Napoleon, later Emperor Napoleon III, appeared armoured and plumed. All these attended banquets, balls, jousts, tilting and the mock-battle or *mêlée*. But the series of cavalcades and the general medievalism of the occasion also attracted goggling thousands of ordinary spectators, marvelling at the antics of their betters. They arrived on roads choked with carriage traffic, and by special excursion trains from Glasgow, to be soaked to the skin, as the toffs were to the silks beneath their coats of mail. The Earl of Eglinton, Lord of the Tournament, bravely declared: 'We command all things here but the weather.'

The Eglinton Tournament (London, 1843)
FB. el. 29

14.14 **Fitba**

A WEST OF SCOTLAND 'tournament' of a rather different kind was recorded by Hiram Sturdy (cf. 4.17) in one of his sketchbooks. This page illustrates an everyday happening; football in the village street of Newarthill. The lower image is of a rarer event, the village fête or sports-day, with a brass band, dancing, stalls for food and drink, and athletics taking place on the makeshift sports-field. This scene captures the essence of what Sturdy expressed simply as 'the village', meaning its spirit, and the sense of being a community or even a big family. Scottish sport is socially stratified, and its various records are keenly collected by the Library. Football has traditionally been a working-class sport, both in the playing and the watching. Rugby is (or was) middle-class. Golf is more élitist, because of the fees and its club life; and some golf is much more élitist than the rest. Mountaineering (particularly when those Scots who climbed had to go abroad to do it) was once very much more select than it is now. Fishing, shooting and stalking retain their upper-class image, as does sailing. Curling unites all. Scottish cricket is just odd.

Dep. 279/19

The writer of the small group of illustrated letters to which this example belongs appears to have been named Wilson. He chose to use a pseudonym, 'Hall Tweed', in composing these playful and flirtatious epistles to the wife of a London physician. He was temporarily resident in Glasgow and its vicinity in the second decade of the nineteenth century. His accounts of local life and manners are enlivened by wickedly witty sketches of the foibles of a city much enriched by trade and manufacturing, and anxious to be up-sides with Edinburgh and even London. 'You have no idea of the Fopping & Foolery exhibited in this town. Altho' 400 miles from Bond Street they far excel the

walking beauties there in nakedness & *outré* dresses. I felt myself no way in humour to go out in the evening, particularly as the ladies were well attended, and after a great deal of abuse and putting about they departed… on honour I am not very wide of their exact dress, as also a Glasgow male Adonis who was in their train. Upon my soul, the ladies in Glasgow will if they go much further leave nothing to dream about, for they are approaching fast to Mother Eve.' The illustration shows the outlandish Regency fashions 'Hall Tweed' describes as 'the Gape, the Stare and the Go of Glasgow'.

Acc. 11842

14.16 The world's first photographic society

THE EDINBURGH CALOTYPE CLUB, formed about 1843, was the world's oldest photographic society, and the albums which its members compiled may constitute the earliest known photograph albums. The appearance of these on the auction market in 2001 caused great excitement, and the Library bought them in partnership with Edinburgh City Libraries: each institution holds one. Photography was a very 'Scottish' scientific art. The names of Hill and Adamson are world-famous as professional photographic pioneers, as is that of the great scientist Sir David Brewster, a friend of William Henry Fox Talbot. But there were also many amateur practitioners whose efforts are recorded here. Some were introduced to the process by Brewster. Calotype photography could be pursued seriously in Scotland because Fox Talbot's patent, taken out in

England in 1841 to protect his process, did not apply in Scotland. Technical advances in photography soon rendered the calotype process redundant, and in 1856 the club made way for the new Photographic Society of Scotland. But its achievement lives on in this album, which contains some of the earliest photographic images of Scotland, its buildings and scenery, and of Scots in their stove-pipe hats, tartan dresses, rusty coats and wrinkled trousers. The man on the left, James Coventry, was an Edinburgh solicitor; the other is James Francis Montgomery, an advocate and later an Episcopalian clergyman, who took this photographic double-portrait. It was his visit to Brewster in St Andrews that sparked the foundation of the Calotype Club.

Phot. Med. 33, acquired with the aid of the Art Fund and the Heritage Lottery Fund

14.17 A Victorian road accident

ACCORDING TO John Francis Campbell of Islay (cf.14.2), in one of whose albums it was found, this dramatic scene is the work of his friend Kirkman Finlay, scion of a prominent Glasgow tea and textile family. It was sent to Campbell by the Duke of Argyll, and allegedly represents an accident experienced by Lord and Lady Amberley, perhaps on the way to Inveraray, in 1865. But Campbell's note appended to the sketch indicates that it actually relates to (and perhaps elaborates upon) an adventure of Finlay's own. Be that as it may, it indicates the hazards of road travel before the arrival of the 'horseless carriage' made things more dangerous still.

Campbell of Islay Papers, Adv. MS. 50.4.2, f. 130

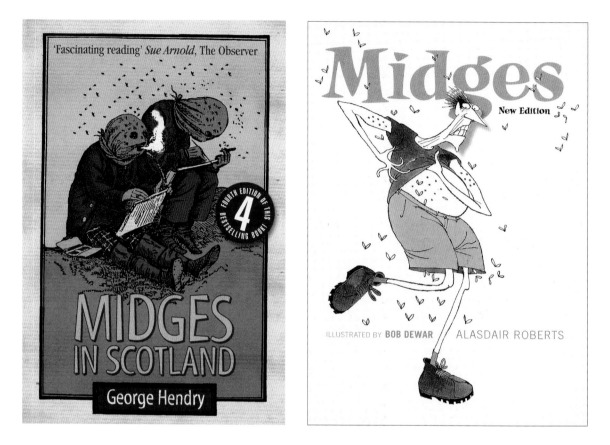

14.18 **Damned midges!**

IN THE LONG CATALOGUE of Scottish villains, *Culicoides impunctatus* ranks high and prominent. Its presence, at first annoying and eventually painful, had been the subject of comment since at least the earlier eighteenth century. It is no respecter of rank, and cares nothing for politics: both Bonnie Prince Charlie and Queen Victoria suffered in their days (and stays). So characteristic is it of Scotland, in what passes for the Scottish summer, that tourists actually like to buy books about it. Two recent authors have bitten into the market with these successful publications: you want a book on midges and then, as with buses, two come along! George Hendry has priority, and (by a long measure) scientific edge. Alasdair Roberts and his illustrator Bob Dewar are lighter on fact but heavier in humour. Both can be used to swat the damned things when they ruin the picnic or the evening drink in the garden.

GEORGE HENDRY, *Midges in Scotland*, 4th edition (Edinburgh, 2003)
PB2. 205.20/10
ALASDAIR ROBERTS and BOB DEWAR, *Midges*, new edition
(Edinburgh, 2005)
PB5. 206.152/9

14.19 You're never lost with a Bartholomew

THE ARCHIVE OF the great cartographic firm of John Bartholomew includes a series of appealing, and very striking, advertising posters for the maps that were to be found in the glove-box of half the motor cars in Britain between the 1920s and the 1970s. The series relied on excellent and dramatic lighting, together with subtle use of props and costume, to convey a sense of wonder and adventure – even if the actual setting were only Surrey or Argyllshire. In the posters an archetypical 1930s middle-class couple, with or without a male friend who appears rather awkwardly out-of-place in company with the contented married pair, consult maps spread beside tents before bedtime, or (as here) over the bonnet of the car, in an effort to locate their position on a pre-'sat nav' summer night's drive.

Bartholomew Archive Acc. 10222/Business Record/1869

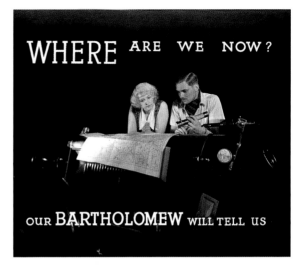

14.20 A Scotsman's home

IT MAY NOT BE a castle; nor the Highland croft of sentimental Edwardian postcards or of *Brigadoon*; nor the 'but-and-ben' to which the Broons of Dudley D. Watkins's famous comic strip retired from Glasgow when in need of some country rest and recreation; nor yet the comfortable house in Edinburgh's Queen Street where the Allan and Harden families lived and created an illustrated epistolary record which constitutes a uniquely important source of evidence for Scottish domestic life (cf. 8.8). But home is home, wherever and whatever it is. Here Hiram Sturdy (cf. 4.17)

shows exhausted miners washing and relaxing in the living-room of a pit-village cottage, with its cast-iron range, kettle on the hob, cauldron suspended on a swey over the coal fire in the grate, and a tap for hot water from the tank beside the fire. A 'wally dug' glazed earthenware fairing ornaments the mantelshelf. The aspidistra is in its pot. The sampler says it all: 'Home Sweet Home'. And the National Library of Scotland is home too: home to the record of Scottish life, of history, of literature, through all time and over all the world.

Dep. 279/ 33

First published in 2010 by
Scala Publishers Ltd
Northburgh House
10 Northburgh Street
London EC1V 0AT
Telephone: +44 (0)20 7490 9900
www.scalapublishers.com

ISBN 978-1-85759-638-0

Project Editor: Jessica Hodge
Designer: Nigel Soper
Produced by Scala Publishers
Printed in China

The author and publishers are grateful to the following copyright holders for permission to reproduce the images listed:

3.8 Church of Scotland; 4.3 Thomson Gale (Charles Scribner's
Sons); 4.17, 8.8, 14.3, 14.14, 14.20 Sturdy family; 4.18 H.R.
Prince; 5.8 Sir Frank Mears Associates, Edinburgh; 5.9 A.P.
Watt Ltd; 6.11 Martin Haldane of Gleneagles; 8.3 and 8.4 with
acknowledgement to the depositor, The Royal Society of
Edinburgh; 10.4 with acknowledgement to the depositor, the
National Galleries of Scotland; 10.10 Kulgin Duval and Colin
Hamilton; 10.11 Mrs Susan Vereker and the Society of Authors
(Shaw Estate); 10.12 © Copyright Administration Ltd 2010;
10.13 Alasdair Gray; 14.5 Christopher Ellice; 14.7 Appletree
Press, with acknowledgement to Clare Hewitt; Deedee
Cuddihy; 14.8 John Dewar & Sons Ltd; 14.18 Birlinn Ltd

Author's acknowledgements

Colleagues across the Library have responded to
my requests for suggestions for items that might be
included in this anthology, and I am conscious that
all too few of those suggestions could be heeded.
I am nonetheless grateful for the stimulus of
discussion, the hint of direction and the answered
question, the confirmation of views and even the
spirited yet comradely disagreement over priorities.
Errors of fact and eccentricities of opinion are mine
alone. Those to whom I am indebted include:
Almut Boehme, John Bowles, Dr Maria Castrillo,
Kenneth Dunn, Christopher Fleet, Olive Geddes,
Dr Anette Hagan, Sally Harrower, Dr Brian Hillyard,
Dr Graham Hogg, Dr Ulrike Hogg, Andrew Martin,
David McClay, Sheila Mackenzie, Alison Metcalfe,
James Mitchell, Robin Smith and Jan Usher. I am
also obliged to the following for assistance of more
practical kinds: Karla Baker, Rachel Beattie, Robert
Betteridge, Alison Buckley, Jennifer Giles, Kevin
Halliwell, Lynn King, Alex O'Hara, Derek Oliver,
Stephen Rigden, Yvonne Shand, George Stanley,
Gwenan Wiley and, not least, the 'bookfetchers' who
(without too much audible cursing) retrieved and
delivered hundreds of volumes large or small for my
inspection. Julian Stone was an ally from the start.

Special thanks go to members of the Reprographic
Unit: Steve McAvoy, Adrian Fowler, George
Morrison and, above all, Robert James, who almost
single-handedly made all the digital images for
this book.

The National Librarian and Chief Executive,
Martyn Wade, and the Senior Management Team,
in particular Cate Newton and Teri Wishart,
have supported this project throughout, as have
Professor Michael Anderson, Chairman, and
members of the Board of Trustees. I thank them
all for their confidence.

It has been a pleasure to work with Scala and its
efficient and cheerful team: Jenny McKinley
(from whom the approach to write this book came),
Oliver Craske, Nigel Soper and especially my
perceptive, good-humoured and patient editor,
Jessica Hodge.

At home, my wife (as Dr Patricia Andrew, a regular
and devoted user of the Library – where first we
met) helped immeasurably in more ways than I can
say, or adequately acknowledge.